About the Author

Heather Heath Dismore is a veteran *For Dummies* author and editor. Her published works include such titles as *Running a Restaurant For Dummies, Indian Cooking For Dummies* (part of the compilation *Cooking Around the World For Dummies All-In-One*), *The Parents' Success Guide to Organizing,* and *The Parents' Success Guide to Managing a Household,* all published by Wiley. She also contributed to *Low Carb Dieting For Dummies.* This is her sixth published work.

Heather graduated from DePauw University with majors in political science and English composition. She started making jewelry for friends and family during college as a way to give beautiful gifts on a limited budget, and she has kept it up for the last 12 years, even though her budget has increased (slightly). She started her company, PageOne Publishing, a growing freelance enterprise focusing on project-based writing, editing, and Web site development, in 2001. She can be contacted at pageonepublishing@yahoo.com.

Heather lives in Missouri with her husband, Andrew Dismore, and their daughters, who are Heather's first loves, inspiration, and never-ending source of new material.

About the Creative Consultant

Tammy Powley is a writer and mixed-media artist. She is the author of *Making Designer Gemstone and Pearl Jewelry* and *Making Designer Bead and Wire Jewelry,* is the co-author of *Art of Jewelry Making,* and has been the Internet Guide for the About.com Jewelry-making Web site at http://jewelry making.about.com since 1998. Tammy has been published in various print publications, including *Jewelry Crafts Magazine, Bead Step-by-Step, Art Jewelry,* and *Kid's Step-by-Step.* In addition to studying a large variety of jewelry techniques, from beading to metalsmithing, she has worked extensively with glass, fiber, and paper art. After spending eight years on the art-show circuit, Tammy eventually turned to writing about art, though she continues to sell her work through special commissions and galleries.

Tammy currently resides in Port St. Lucie, Florida, with her husband, Michael, and a house full of dogs and cats.

Dedication

I dedicate this book to my grandmother, Anna Mae Dyess, who started my love of jewelry with a bottomless box of costume jewelry, open to all her grandchildren to create what they would. You are loved and missed, but not forgotten.

Author's Acknowledgments

A special thank you to Tammy Powley. Her creativity, insights, and incredible talent helped make this book terrific. She contributed many of the beautiful projects you see in this book. Her quick and tireless review of chapters, pictures, and never-ending project instructions were fantastic and much appreciated.

Thanks to Tere Drenth, my amazing project editor, who kept this project on track despite many stops and starts; too many graphics, pictures, and illustrations to count; and other inevitable challenges along the way. Always a pleasure to work with you, my friend!

Thanks to the whole team at Fire Mountain Gems, including Sue Zimmerman, David Anderson, Todd Bushman, and John Parrish. They contributed supplies for projects, cool graphics of beads and more, and a collective sense of humor that makes them a joy to work with.

Thank you to everyone at Wiley who made this book a success, including Diane Steele, Joyce Pepple, Kristin Cocks, Tracy Boggier, Carmen Krikorian, Laura Moss, Maridee Ennis, Barbara Moore, Lynsey Osborn, Brian Drumm, and many other behind-the-scenes folks in the editorial and production departments. As always, thanks for the opportunity to work with the best in the business.

Thanks also to my incredible family for their patience and support during the never-ending writing schedule.

Publisher's Acknowledgments

We're proud of this book; please send us your comments through our Dummies online registration form located at www.dummies.com/register/.

Some of the people who helped bring this book to market include the following:

*Acquisitions, Editorial, and
Media Development*

Project Editor: Tere Stouffer Drenth

Acquisitions Editor: Tracy Boggier

Technical Reviewer: J.S. Dunn

Editorial Manager: Carmen Krikorian

Editorial Assistant: Nadine Bell

Cover Photos: ©Getty Images/ThinkStock

Cartoons: Rich Tennant, www.the5thwave.com

Composition

Project Coordinator: Maridee Ennis

Layout and Graphics: Jonelle Burns, Kelly Emkow, Lauren Goddard, Joyce Haughey, Stephanie D. Jumper, Barbara Moore, Barry Offringa, Lynsey Osborn, Jacque Roth, Rashell Smith, Julie Trippetti

Proofreaders: Joe Niesen, TECHBOOKS Publishing Services

Indexer: TECHBOOKS Publishing Services

Publishing and Editorial for Consumer Dummies

> **Diane Graves Steele,** Vice President and Publisher, Consumer Dummies

> **Joyce Pepple,** Acquisitions Director, Consumer Dummies

> **Kristin A. Cocks,** Product Development Director, Consumer Dummies

> **Michael Spring,** Vice President and Publisher, Travel

> **Brice Gosnell,** Associate Publisher, Travel

> **Kelly Regan,** Editorial Director, Travel

Publishing for Technology Dummies

> **Andy Cummings,** Vice President and Publisher, Dummies Technology/General User

Composition Services

> **Gerry Fahey,** Vice President of Production Services

> **Debbie Stailey,** Director of Composition Services

Contents at a Glance

Table of Contents

Introduction

•   •

*J*ewelry making and beading is not only for the professionals. It's a terrific way to express your artistic and creative side, quickly and easily. In practically no time, you can make simple, elegant jewelry.

Jewelry making is a hobby for anyone. Whether you're a painter, accountant, or stay-at-home mom, you can participate in and excel at jewelry making and beading. If you can string a single bead, you can make jewelry. And after you get started, you can stick with the basics or improve your skills further. In fact, in a short time, you can move from hobby to business.

You can't find any better way to spend an afternoon than sorting and sifting through containers of beads, vintage jewelry components, threads, cord, and other fun materials. Find your local bead store (see Chapter 3 for tips on finding your local store) and decide for yourself.

About This Book

I wrote this book to show you how easy and fun jewelry making and beading is. This book introduces all of the basic jewelry-making techniques, like stringing beads, knotting thread, wrapping wire, and working with polymer clay, giving you hands-on projects along the way. I give you easy-to-follow instructions, complete with illustrations and pictures where you need them.

I also spend some time discussing design principles, so that you can develop your own unique projects. With many of the projects, I give you suggestions for varying the designs and components, so when you're ready, you can make each piece your own.

Conventions Used in This Book

To help you navigate through this book, I use the following conventions:

✔ *Italics* are used for emphasis and to highlight new words or terms that are defined.

✔ Monofont is used for Web addresses. Note that when this book was printed, some Web addresses may have needed to break across two lines of text. If that happened, rest assured that I haven't put in any extra characters (such as hyphens) to indicate the break. So, when using one of these Web addresses, just type in exactly what you see in this book, pretending the line break doesn't exist.

✔ Sidebars, which look like text enclosed in a shaded gray box, give you information that's interesting to know but not necessarily critical to your understanding of the chapter or section topic.

✔ Projects are numbered for your convenience, using the Chapter number and relative number of the project in the chapter. So, for example, Project 3-2, is the second project in Chapter 3.

✔ The word *findings* is used quite a bit in this book and it refers to jewelry-making elements that help you connect, embellish, finish, and start projects. Check out Chapter 2 to get the full scoop on findings and other jewelry-making necessities.

Foolish Assumptions

Despite the well-known pitfalls of making assumptions, I've made a few of my own while writing this book. If any of these describe you perfectly or hit close to home, this book may be just what you're looking for:

✔ You like jewelry and own a few of your own pieces.

✔ You've made jewelry as gifts for friends or family members and want to discover some new techniques and tricks to jazz up your next gift-giving season.

✔ You're looking for a relaxing, creative hobby.

✔ You have a little extra cash and want to trade it in for plastic boxes full of beads.

✔ You want to wear trendy, hip jewelry but don't have the bank account to support it.

How This Book Is Organized

This book is organized into several different parts, just like my bead organizer. Here's what's in each compartment.

Part I: Creating Irresistible Jewelry

In this part, I introduce you to the world of jewelry making and beading. I give you a general overview of the tools and supplies you need to get started, with tips on what to buy now and what to buy later. I give you the lowdown on setting up your jeweler's toolbox and help you decide where to set up your workspace. I make sure you're in the know about the differences between all the wires, cords, threads, and other materials available in jewelry supply outlets today. I also show you basic bead shapes and styles and included tips on how to put them together. And I get you going with several starter projects.

Part II: Discovering Simple Jewelry-Making Techniques

In Part II, I focus on showing you the ropes (well, actually cord, threads, and wire) of many jewelry-making techniques, like stringing and knotting, weaving and looming, and working with wire. I break up the part into chapters focused on different techniques, and each chapter includes several great projects to practice the specific technique as you go. But you can skip around any time you want, especially if one particular technique catches your fancy.

Part III: Implementing Design Ideas, Trends, and More

In this part, I build on the techniques I show you in Part II. This part is full of projects (more than 60 in all) with complete step-by-step instructions, illustrations, and photos to show you how create these beautiful pieces on your own. I give you tips for varying the projects, based on your budgets and preferences.

I break up the chapters by themes. Work through them in whatever order seems to interest you. Look here for chapters on special-occasion jewelry and great trendy, everyday designs. And don't miss the tips on adding touches to your designs to reflect particular ethnic influences or to conjure up a feeling for a particular time period.

Part IV: Building On Your Jewelry-Making Hobby

Look to this part when you're ready to start thinking about the next steps for your fun new hobby. Here, I give you ideas for using jewelry-making techniques for decorating your home. I also show you how to host a jewelry-making party and how to make jewelry with kids. And I show you how to start a jewelry-making business, whether you want to simply sell a few pieces or open your own full-fledged shop.

Part V: The Part of Tens

This part gives you just the facts, ma'am. I give you my ten favorite online resources for jewelry making. I also give you a heads-up about ten common mistakes to avoid while still enjoying your new hobby. And finally, I show you ten great ways to make money with your new talent because, hey, even if you break even, you still get to bead for free!

Icons Used in This Book

Icons are the fancy little pictures in the margins of this book. Here's the guide to what they mean and what the icons look like:

This icon marks suggestions that can make a technique or project a bit easier. The tips are usually hands-on ways to improve your designs and finished projects.

This icon points out ideas that sum up and reinforce the concepts I discuss. In fact, if you're in a time crunch and can't read an entire section, go straight to this icon.

This icon to alert you to potential pitfalls and to give you a heads-up on what mistakes to avoid. Pay particular attention when this icon rears its head; it could save you time and money.

Think of this icon as bonus material — the info by this icons gives you some background about the subject that's not critical. I think it's interesting, so I include it, but you don't have to read the material to understand the techniques and projects.

Where to Go from Here

If you're like me, when you see projects that interest you, you just have to stop, grab your pliers and make something. (In fact, the hardest part of working on this book is putting down the pliers to write down all the fun stuff I'm working on.) Or, you may sit in a comfortable chair and read this book from cover to cover.

But one of the great things about a *For Dummies* book (among the hundreds that I can count) is that you don't have to read it word for word, front to back, cover to cover. If you're more interested in one particular topic than another, that's fine. Check out the corresponding part, chapter, or section and read up on that technique or project. You can find out about it without first having read the information that precedes it — get-in-and-get-out convenience. Interested in tips to make jewelry with kids? Turn to Chapter 13. Do you need help honing your wire wrapping technique? Check out Chapter 7. Want the full story on setting up your workspace? Chapter 4 has your name written all over it.

You can jump around, start wherever you want, and finish when you feel like it. So grab your pliers and get going.

Part I

Creating Irresistible Jewelry

The 5th Wave   By Rich Tennant

"I try not to be offended when Paige and
her friends want to look through my closet
because they're making 'antique' jewelry."

In this part . . .

Get ready to start making jewelry, all kinds of beautiful jewelry. In fact, you can finish your first project before you finish Chapter 1. In this part, I introduce you to the basic tools and supplies you need to have in your beginner's toolbox. I also help you decide where to set it all up, ideally in a separate space in your home dedicated to the fine art of making jewelry. This part is your guide to all the basics of bead shapes and sizes and wire shapes, as well as gauges, threads, cords, and other stringing materials. You get all this information plus a great sampling of beginner projects to get you started making jewelry in no time.

Chapter 1

An Insider's Look at Jewelry Making and Beading

In This Chapter

▶ Deciding whether jewelry-making is for you

▶ Introducing jewelry-making techniques

▶ Choosing your projects

▶ Making more from your jewelry-making hobby

Although I could spend time explaining how rewarding, creative, and fun jewelry making and beading are, I'll show you instead. Flip to the color photo section near the middle of this book, filled with beautiful, glossy photos of handmade jewelry pieces. Just flip through it, look at some of the projects there, and come on back to this chapter when you're ready. Go ahead, I'll wait.

Like what you see? I spend the rest of the book giving you details on how to make each and every piece you see in the color *and* black-and-white pages of this book.

In this chapter, I give you an overview of the topics, techniques, and projects that I cover in the book, and I help you start making jewelry on your own using a variety of techniques that you can apply to the 65 projects throughout this book. I also give you plenty of tips for taking these techniques and adapting them to create your own designs. And finally, I give you ideas for making money with your newfound hobby. While reading, feel free to take a break at any time, whip out your pliers and bead something.

Why Make Jewelry Yourself?

The best reason to make jewelry yourself is pure enjoyment. Pure artistic, creative energy pouring into your creation is incredibly satisfying. But this creativity has a practical side, too: something to wear. You can make very simple quick pieces to wear today, or you can create complicated designs that take hours, even days to complete. You're in charge and limited only by your imagination.

Here are a few of my other favorite reasons for making jewelry:

- ✔ You can create one-of-a-kind pieces that no one else has.
- ✔ You can make inexpensive, beautiful gifts for your family and friends.
- ✔ You want to spend hours culling through strings, strands, and bins or beautiful beads.
- ✔ You have tons of divided plastic containers and don't know what to do with them.
- ✔ You can't fathom giving Paris Hilton (heiress, model, reality TV star, actress, singer, and brand new jewelry designer) any more money.
- ✔ You can start a low-cost home-based business.
- ✔ You can always find a new technique, stitch, or pattern that you haven't tried before, which means you can't reach the end of everything there is to know about this hobby.

Finding ways to inspire your creativity

Where you go with your newfound hobby is entirely up to you. You choose where your interest lies, what techniques and pieces to develop, and what to do with your pieces when you're done. Let your creativity be your guide.

If you're still looking for ways to get the creative juices flowing, consider the following:

- ✔ **Go to your library or bookstore.** Look at any jewelry-making books you can find. Even if a particular book focuses on a technique you don't think you'll ever try, it's worth spending time looking at them. You can get countless ideas from just looking at what other people have done.

  Check to see whether your local library has an online catalog at its Web site. Often, a library's catalog ties into other systems that let you borrow a book not available in your area through an interlibrary loan program. Some search terms for jewelry-making inspirations include: jewelry making, jewelry trends, bead, beading, bead making, embellish, bead weaving, fashion, jewelry design, design, home décor, and crafts.

  Don't look only in the adult section (and I don't mean the smutty one!) at your library or bookstore. Check out the kid's craft areas, too, where you can find great resources that can provide inspiration.

- ✔ **Search the Internet.** Look up different styles of jewelry, search for ancient inspirations and the hottest trends, or look up specific terms like "bead weaving patterns" or "tin cup necklace" and you're sure to get some inspiring pictures, techniques, and tutorials. Also take a look at celebrity "news" sites like www.eonline.com to see what the stars think is hot. And check out huge shopping sites like Amazon.com (www.amazon.com). Amazon doesn't show you the cutting edge of jewelry design, but you can look at the current fashion trends.

✔ **Subscribe to a jewelry making or beading magazine.** A library is a great place to get a sampling of jewelry-making magazines. But getting your own copy in the mail on a regular basis is a boon to your creative energy.

✔ **Order a catalog from a large bead and jewelry supply house.** Catalogs are like carrying a bead store with you! My personal favorite is Fire Mountain Gems and Beads; I like its catalog because it has plenty of project ideas mixed with fantastic full-color photos throughout the catalog. Every time I pickup the catalog, I want to make several somethings. Visit Fire Mountain's Web site at www.firemountaingems.com and click on catalog request. Or call the customer service number (800-423-2319) to request a free 500+ page catalog. Check out the ad in the back of this book for a special offer just for you.

✔ **Spend a few hours in a bead store.** Ultimately, there's no better way to get inspired right now than to walk into your local bead store. Feel the beads. Hold them in your hand. Walk around with them. Hold them next to other beads. Lay them out on a bead board. Some stores actually have tools to make your pieces right there in the store. Check out Chapter 3 for design tips and ideas on pairing beads together.

You'll never spend just a short time in a bead store, so allow plenty of time to wander, explore, and create.

Deciding whether to set up a separate workspace

Should you set up a separate jewelry-making workspace? In a word: probably. How's that for definite? But seriously, setting up a workspace just for making jewelry has many benefits. Here are just a few of those benefits:

✔ **You control the noise level.** If you like to work to music, blare it. If you don't, don't even keep a radio in your space. By having your own workspace, you can also keep other people from making noise in your space when you want a quiet atmosphere.

✔ **You control the light level.** If you're trying to make jewelry in the same area that someone else is trying to meditate, read, or do homework, your lighting needs may not take priority. In your own space, you're the boss.

✔ **You control the activity level.** You may have difficulty being creative and satisfied when people are milling around, asking you questions, or if the phone is ringing. Or maybe for you, having activity around you isn't a problem. You can locate your workspace outside (or inside) the flow of everything else going on in your house.

✔ **You can leave a half-finished project on a bead board, covered of course, without being in anyone's way.** Because jewelry making is fun for everyone, you'll have no shortage of curious onlookers. Accidents can happen when they look, though, and a separate workspace keeps unfinished projects with loose beads away from prying eyes and exploring hands.

✔ **You can lock your door.** A little added security maybe just what you need to complete your masterpiece. You decide what you need in your space. Just having a door is helpful, but a lock is that much safer.

Are you sensing a pattern here?

Ultimately, having a separate studio or office for making jewelry is ideal. But don't let the fact that you don't or can't have one right now keep you from getting started. Check out Chapter 4 for tips on making the most out of whatever space you do have.

Discovering Jewelry-Making Designs and Techniques

I intersperse design tips and tricks throughout this book. For many of the projects, I give you ideas for making the project your own. When appropriate, I also give you patterns to follow and always provide illustrations.

The following sections briefly explain simple jewelry-making techniques. You can get the lowdown on each in Part II.

Stringing and knotting

Stringing, threading beads onto a cord or thread, is the first technique most jewelry makers start with. In fact, you can get started with stringing in this very chapter in Project 1-1 in the last section of this chapter. Techniques for stringing beads and connecting jewelry findings are used in some way or another in just about every single piece of jewelry.

Knotting, tying knots between beads, is traditionally used to separate fine gemstones, like pearls, on simple elegant strands. But trendy pieces like the Tin Cup Necklace (see Chapter 5) can be made with this technique as well.

Bead weaving

Bead weaving is sort of like stringing and knotting together. Using a needle and thread, you string beads, and then tie knots through beads and through threads connecting beads to reveal elaborate, often delicate designs. For the full story, take a look at Chapter 6.

Wire wrapping

Wire wrapping is twisting and bending wire into shapes or around beads. This technique is exciting because you can do just about anything with it. Create delicate chains, beautiful wrapped beads, or easy dangle earrings. Look to Chapter 7 for exciting and easy designs using this technique.

Putting a few techniques to use

Project 1-1, a Celtic Knot Pendant on Leather Cord, gives you a chance to try some simple jewelry-making techniques.

Project 1-1: Celtic Knot Pendant on Leather Cord

You use a simple sterling silver Celtic knot pendant in this design. If you have a different favorite pendant (like a wolf, bear, arrowhead, or cross, for example), feel free to substitute. And if leather isn't your thing, a hemp or silk cord can also display a beautiful single pendant. Take a look at Chapter 2 if you need help with any of the tools or supplies. Check out Figure 1-3 to see the finished project.

Tools and Materials

Round nosed pliers	*Celtic pendant, sterling silver*
2 feet black leather cord, 2mm round	*2 coil-end lobster claw clasp*

1. **String the pendant onto the cord.**

   Yours should look something like Figure 1-1.

2. **Holding your cord (with pendant attached) in one hand, take the clasp in the other. Insert the end of your cord into one coil end of your clasp.**

   Take a look at Figure 1-2a.

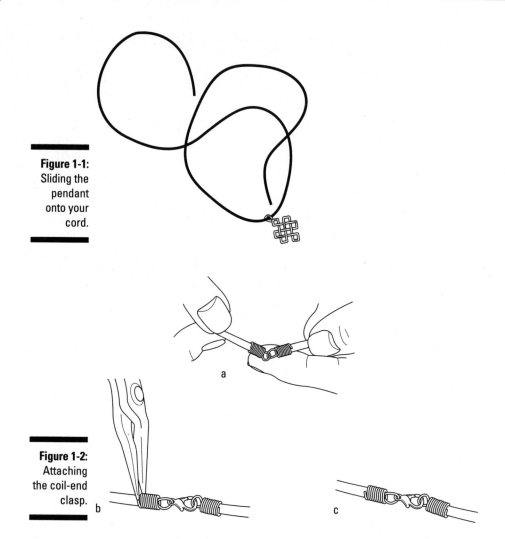

Figure 1-1:
Sliding the
pendant
onto your
cord.

Figure 1-2:
Attaching
the coil-end
clasp.

3. **Using the round-nose pliers, pinch the coil end around your leather cord, as shown in Figure 1-2b.**

   Use your pliers to bend the last coil in the clasp, instead of trying to mash the entire end of the clasp flat.

4. **Repeat Steps 2 and 3 to finish the other side of your clasp.**

   The finished clasp should look like Figure 1-2c.

Figure 1-3:
Celtic Knot
Pendant on
Leather
Cord.

From Antique to Funky: Creating Innovative Jewelry

Jewelry isn't just for special occasions. Whatever your style and interest, with more than 70 projects in this book, you can make pieces that you can wear or use everyday. The tough part is deciding which projects to make first.

Here are a few suggestions for how to prioritize your project list:

- **Stretchy beaded bracelets:** Bracelets created without a clasp on a continuous elastic band are extremely popular right now. You can find several bracelets with different bead combinations in Chapter 5 (Project 5-1), Chapter 8 (Project 8-6), and Chapter 9 (Project 9-10). Take a look at Figure 1-4 to see each project.

- **Y-necklaces:** A Y-necklace takes its name from the distinctive Y-shape made by the necklace and dangle. Take your pick from Projects 8-5 and 10-1, in Chapter 8 and 9, respectively. You can see each project in Figure 1-5.

Figure 1-4:
Stretchy
bracelets.

Figure 1-5:
Y-necklaces.

✔ **Illusion necklace:** Illusion necklaces are those sparsely beaded necklaces strung on invisible thread that give the illusion that the beads are floating on your neck by themselves. You can find a version in Chapter 2 (Project 2-1). Check out Figure 1-6 to see it up close.

✔ **Hip, simple earrings:** Try the Psimple Psychedelic Earrings in Chapter 11 (Project 11-5) or the Wrapped Beaded Earrings in Chapter 7 (Project 7-3), both shown in Figure 1-7. And of course, I put a whole slew of earring projects in their very own section in Chapter 8.

✔ **Asian inspired necklace and earring set:** Get some good karma with this Asian-influenced jewelry set. Take a look at Figure 1-8 and get the full instructions and helpful illustrations in Chapter 10 (Project 10-3).

Don't miss the themed chapters in Part III, where you find, among other things, a chapter on completing retro-inspired projects (see Chapter 11). Also check out Chapter 12 in Part IV, in which you create home décor accents that utilize jewelry-making techniques and beading.

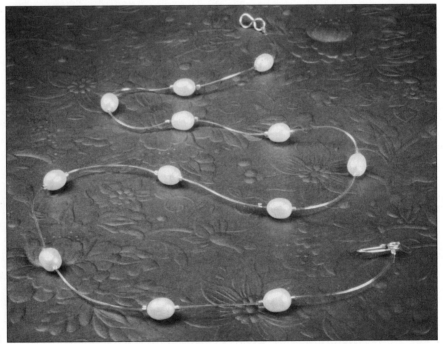

Figure 1-6: Illusion Necklace.

Figure 1-7:
Simple
earrings.

Figure 1-8:
Asian
Inspired
Good-Luck
Necklace
and
Earrings.

Taking Your Hobby to the Next Level

When do you know you're addicted to jewelry making and beading? When you just can't help but share it with everyone else. It's hard to resist when people compliment you on your pieces or your kids (and their friends) want to get into your bead bins.

You can involve other people (assuming you want to) in your hobby in many ways. Here are a few favorites:

- ✔ **Try a new technique with a friend.** If she's a wire wrapper and you're an experienced bead stringer, take a bead-making class together. Often, the most interesting and innovative pieces of jewelry employed several jewelry-making techniques. Part II introduces all the techniques used in this book.

- ✔ **Host a jewelry-making party for your friends.** I show you how to set it up, whom to invite, and how to organize a great party. Check out Chapter 14 for details.

- ✔ **Make jewelry with kids.** In Chapter 13, I give you step-by-step support for choosing the best projects for each age group, keeping everyone interested and on task. Your kids will complete beautiful projects everyone can be proud of.

- ✔ **Sell your pieces and your expertise.** You can make money selling your jewelry and your talent. Whether you're sitting at your own booth at an art show or posting your pieces on the Internet, you can find a market for your pieces. In Chapter 15, I help you work through the legal and logistical issues to find a way to make it work for you including finding classes that you can teach and shows where you can exhibit.

Chapter 2

Tricks and Tools of the Trade

. . . .

. . . .

*W*ant to discover the tools and tricks of professional jewelry makers? You've come to the right place. In this chapter, I show you how to choose the right stringing materials (thread, cord, wire, and so on) to work with the designs you like. I also show you which pliers are must-haves for every jewelry maker. I even help you convert to and from the pesky metric system to make sure you buy the right amount of supplies. Finally, I show you how to choose just the right hardware to finish your jewelry pieces with style.

This chapter is your guide to getting your tools and basic supplies together so that you can make the jewelry you've always dreamed of making. When you're ready to buy pearls, beads, and stones, take a look at Chapter 3.

Stringing You Along with Threads, Cords, and Wire

Stringing beads is one of the most basic techniques in jewelry making, but the basics can quickly get complicated by trade names, different widths, diameters and other measurements, and so on. In this section, I help you sort through three categories of must-have supplies: threads, cords, and wire.

Unraveling threads

A *thread* is a thin strand of material used to connect, string, or tie jewelry together. Many different types of threads are used for different types of projects with different kinds of beads. I highlight many of my favorites and give you tips for using them successfully in your own designs.

Thread *weights* (thread weight is shorthand for the amount of weight a thread can hold without breaking) aren't very intuitive, and not all threads are available in all weights. Here's the range, from light to heavy weight, which means smallest to largest diameter: OO, O, A, B, C, D, E, F, FF, FFF. In general, the higher the thread weight, the larger the diameter or width of the thread. Some brands of thread have their own weight labeling systems that use numbers or distinctions like light, medium, or heavy. In most cases, they also provide you with recommendations on what to use for your specific project.

Choose colors to enhance the colors of your transparent or semi-transparent beads. For example, use turquoise thread with clear and turquoise crystals to get even more blue tones into your work. Note that you don't need to match colors, necessarily, just think of colored thread as one more design tool to be explored.

Nylon thread

Often, first-time jewelry makers start out making their first necklaces on fishing line. (I know I did!) When you're first getting started, you may not know that better alternatives are out there.

The only jewelry-making use I recommend for fishing line is to temporarily string beads. (In fact, you'll probably see strands of beads hanging in the bead store on fishing line.) But fishing line isn't strong and tends to either break or warp over time, ruining your pieces and making the jewelry unsuitable to wear.

Nylon thread is a popular beading thread. Tons of colors are available. It's an excellent choice for hard or heavier gem beads, such as rock crystal, agate, and aventurine, as well as with metal beads that can have rougher bead holes that can fray silk or softer cords. It's sold on 20-yard and 100-yard spools without a needle (so you have to buy one separately), or on 2-yard cards with a needle.

Nymo is a colored nylon thread that looks like dental floss. It's most often used with seed beads, the tiny beads used in weaving and clothing designs. (See Chapter 3 for information on specific beads).

If you're starting loomwork or any seed or bugle bead projects, coat your thread with beeswax first. It will keep the thread from fraying and help the finished product last longer. Or you could use Silamide thread that comes prewaxed and twisted (it's also available in tons of colors so you don't have to sacrifice design for convenience). Check out Chapter 6 for the full story on weaving and looming.

Silk

Silk thread is the choice when beading organic gems, like pearls. It's used mostly for fine gems because they seem to flow better on silk thread. It's soft and comes in several colors. I recommend using a lighter weight thread like "B" for knotting 5mm to 6mm gems. Go a littler heavier for larger millimeter beads, or a little lighter for smaller delicate ones.

As a general rule, *hand-knotting* a necklace (or tying knots in between each bead) adds 1 inch to 3 inches to a strand of beads. The length gained is dependent upon the size of the beads and the size of the thread used. So a 16-inch strand of 5mm beads makes a necklace about 18 inches.

Other threads

Kevlar, the same material used to make bulletproof vests, makes a very strong thread. Easy to cut yet impossible to break, Kevlar is perfect for seed bead work, especially if you have some rough beads, like cheaper glass or even crystal, that could cut ordinary thread. It's available in natural yellow and dyed black.

Monofilament thread is a single-strand thread. It's a clear thread designed especially for jewelry making and works well for illusion-style necklaces and other designs where you don't want the thread to show. Look for it at just about any crafts stores in the jewelry-making section as well as from most vendors who sell beading supplies. For beginner's, this is an inexpensive thread, but it's not a huge improvement from fishing line. Use it, but move up to something more durable as soon as you can.

Getting caught up in cord

A *cord* is used much like thread, but cords are generally thicker and, typically, stronger than thread. Cords can be made from traditional materials, like leather or satin, or from technologically advanced products, like stainless steel or nylon.

Elastic cord

Elastic is great for stretchy slip-on jewelry such as bracelets, anklets, watchbands, and children's jewelry. Elastic cord can be knotted and used with beads with a 0.5mm or larger stringing hole. Finish your strands by knotting or with cord caps or cord coils and clasp.

Crimps, beads you bend or smash into place, can tear the cord, but many jewelry makers manage to do it. Practice on scraps before you try to attach one to the creation you've just spent hours on.

Depending on what deigns you're creating, choose colored or clear cord. A few brand names to look for include Stretch Floss, Powercord, Elasticity, and Stretch Magic.

Clear nylon cord

Clear nylon is terrific for making illusion-style necklaces like the one in Project 2-1 at the end of this chapter. It looks like fishing line, but it's woven, so it's much stronger. It's a great choice for clear beads, such as Austrian crystal, where you want little or no cord color to show through. Crimp beads and clamshells work great to finish nylon cord designs. (Check out the "Putting It Together: Choosing and Using Findings" section later in the chapter for more information on crimp beads and other findings.) Nylon cord brand names include C-Thru "Thread," Invisible Bead Cord by Gudebrod, and Supplemax.

I like to use Supplemax for my designs. I think it feels better for the wearer than the generic cord. It works well with glued beads and with crimps. But it doesn't knot very well. Supplemax costs slightly more than the other clear cords, so try it and experiment. Use what works best for you.

Satin cord

Satin cord is loosely woven in three sizes: 2mm (rattail); 1.5mm (mousetail); and 1mm (bugtail). It's available in many colors including metallics, and all of them have a fairly high sheen. Finish the ends of satin cord with cord tips that can be either glued or crimped. I use the red cord in Asian-inspired designs, with metal beads mixed with different-colored jade stones or cloisonné beads (see Chapter 3).

Not all satin cord is colorfast, so if you need to make sure your creation doesn't bleed or fade, read the spool labels closely.

Satin ribbon is often used as a beading cord. It's the same thin, flat ribbon available at your local sewing or crafts supply store. Use the thin, flat linguine-sized organza silk ribbon to string large-hole beads and create easy Victorian chokers. Tie the choker with the ends of the ribbon simply tied in a bow.

Stainless steel

Stainless steel is an excellent material for stringing beads. It's so rigid that you don't need a needle even when stringing smaller beads. But it's flexible enough to hang well and look terrific with large or small beads. It's made of multiple strands of twisted stainless steel, and then coated with nylon. Depending on the weight of the cord, you'll find anywhere from 3 to 49 separate strands to make up a single cord. The more strands, the heavier the weight and the higher the price. Look for brand names like Accu-flex, Acculon, Beadalon, and Soft Flex.

Some manufacturers call their stainless steel stringing material *cable, thread,* or *beading wire,* so don't let that confuse you. Stainless steel doesn't knot well, so I don't call it *thread.* And it doesn't twist or wrap well, so I don't call it *wire.* Whatever you call it, it's a great choice for creating strong bead strands that drape on the body well. Stainless steel cord is sized by the wires diameter, so the thinnest comes in 0.010 inch and the thickest comes in 0.024 inch, depending on the manufacturer.

Leather, pleather

Suede leather cord is made from genuine leather and permanently dyed to maintain color. Look for it in natural shades, like black and brown, and not-so-natural shades, like red, green, or purple. It has a square shape, like a shoelace, and works perfectly for western-style designs that include black, turquoise, or silver beads. Because it's suede, it has a rougher look than leather — making it perfect for more rustic designs.

Remember to look for beads with larger holes when using leather. Typically, the suede lace leather is 3mm wide and the leather is 0.5mm to 3mm wide.

Leather cord is typically a smooth, round cord, but it's also available braided or flat. It is made from genuine leather and permanently dyed so it is colorfast. It is smoother than the rough-looking suede lace cord, but it's used in similar designs, such as bolo ties and other western designs. For a really chic look, wear leather cord around your neck with just a beautiful silver clasp and a strong pendant in the center.

Imitation leather cord, also called *pleather* or *leatherette,* is a woven round cord made from cotton, which looks like leather. It has a more uniform width than animal leather and is surprisingly strong. It's very easy to work with and knots easily. Look for braided bolo ties made from this material.

Imitation leather isn't colorfast, so don't wear it in the pool or shower!

Other cool cords

Consider some other forms of cords:

✔ **Macramé cord** is available in tons of different colors. It resists fraying, threads smoothly and holds knots well. However, it is not colorfast, so it bleeds when washed. Use this for woven projects that won't need to be washed often, such as key chains and potholders.

✔ **Hemp cord** is available in a variety of diameters and package sizes. It's a great choice for making more delicate macramé designs that incorporate beads. It knots easily and maintains shape well under normal wear. The natural color is the most popular and looks great strung with shells or large carved or wooden beads. Look for it in colorfast colors as well to add a splash of color to your designs. Because it is rather thick, use it with larger-hole beads or pendants.

✔ **Crinkled silk cord** takes and holds knots well, is colorfast, and comes in a variety of colors. Because it's basically a thin, hollow tube, you can insert memory wire or elastic through it to make hair scrunchies or skinny headbands. Braid several colors together and tie beads into the braids.

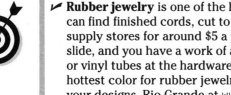

✔ **Rubber jewelry** is one of the hottest trends in jewelry making today. You can find finished cords, cut to length with the clasp attached, at jewelry supply stores for around $5 a piece. Attach your favorite pendant or slide, and you have a work of art. Many jewelry makers buy thin rubber or vinyl tubes at the hardware store to make their own. Black is the hottest color for rubber jewelry, but feel free to use whatever color suits your designs. Rio Grande at `www.riogrande.com` carries a complete line of rubber stringing materials, so order a catalog and get browsing.

Getting strung out on wire

Wire is an essential part of any jewelry maker's supply kit, and it comes in various colors, strengths, widths, and of course, metals. Some wire is sold on bulk spools, and some in little coils.

Because you'll likely be using a lot of wire, always start out with the small coils to figure out exactly what you like to work with. After you've decided what you like for a particular project, you can buy the bulk spools.

Finishing thick cord jewelry

Cord jewelry can be finished in several ways including crimping, knotting, and gluing. Thick cords like leather and rubber tubing aren't quite as versatile, but with a few easy steps you can finish them like a pro.

Tools and Materials

Flat-nose pliers

Length of cord of your choice

Coil-end lobster claw clasp

1. **Feed the cord up into one side of the coil.**

2. **Use your pliers to gently pinch the coil until it's tightened around the cord.**

3. **Repeat Steps 1 and 2 with the other end of the cord.**

This technique is a bit tricky when you're just starting out. Sometimes the coil breaks, so you may have to try this several times before you get the hang of this. Buy a few extra cord materials along with coil-end clasps just for the sake of practicing.

Here are some of my favorite wire choices and how to use them:

✔ **Memory wire** is rigid pre-coiled wire that makes simple and stylish finger and toe rings, bracelets and chokers, and even tiaras. Even when not worn, items made from memory wire retain their round shape and snap back into shape after being stretched. Memory wire is sold in pre-rounded coils like a spring. Just cut off the right number of coils (usually one or two) for your project. Because it's rigid, it's really easy for kids to work with. They can easily slip beads onto the end and quickly make a beautiful work of art. For more on making jewelry with kids, check out Chapter 13.

Choose the diameter of memory wire coil you want to work with:

- • **Ring:** Besides rings and toe rings, this size is also great for wine glass charms. Check out Chapter 12 to make your own wine glass charms.

- • **Bracelet/anklet:** These come in standard (diameter roughly 1.75 to 2.25 inches) and large (diameter roughly 2.25 to 2.63 inches).

- • **Choker/necklace:** This style comes in both standard (diameter roughly 3.6 to 4 inches) and large (diameter roughly 4 to 4.5 inches). Choose whichever size works for your design and whom you're designing it for.

For long-lasting stretch, get the heavier stainless steel Remembrance memory wire by Beadalon that won't rust like ordinary steel memory wire. Check out www.beadalon.com for ordering information. Memory wire is so easy to use — just make a loop on one end, string on beads, and finish your piece with a loop (take a look at Chapter 7 to see how to make a loop) or top the end with a *half-drilled bead* (holes are drilled half way through the bead) or an *end cap* (a half-drilled metal bead). A little touch of glue holds the end cap perfectly. Use either one loop for single-loop designs or more than one loop for multi-loop designs to make cuff bracelets or multi-strand chokers.

When cutting memory wire, hold on to the piece you're cutting off. Otherwise, the piece may shoot off and injure someone. Because memory wire is so hard and rigid, it can damage wire cutters with repeated use. Either use some heavy-duty wire cutters (that you normally wouldn't use for expensive wire like sterling) or better yet, invest in a pair of *memory wire cutters*. Beadalon makes a special set that makes the whole job easier on your hands.

✔ **Super-thin beading wire** is, well, super-thin, 34-gauge wire used for working with tiny beads. Look for it in small gold- and silver-colored spools. Use it for forming shapes in small bead strands or weaving around findings. I've even used it to attach a beaded dangle to a necklace. Use it for lightweight beads only, like bugle or seed beads. See Chapter 3 for the full story on a wide variety of beads, including bugle and seed beads.

Super-thin wire can get quite messy when unraveled (picture a fishing pole with a wad of tangled line), so keep it separated in a resealable plastic bag in the thread section of your tool box.

✔ **Colored wire** is a color-coated copper- or niobium-based crafting wire. Although it comes in several widths, it is soft and extremely malleable and retains shape moderately well. It is ideal for children's crafts and jewelry. Available at any crafts store or online catalog, it comes in several widths and colors ranging from sapphire blue to magenta to black. A 20-yard spool of copper-based colored 24-gauge wire is around $4, and a 5-foot package of niobium-colored wire should run you under $10. If you don't want that much of a single color, consider getting a sampler that contains 10 to15 smaller spools in various colors. It's a great choice for experimenting with color and design.

Many people who work with colored wire use special nylon jaw pliers to prevent nicks and chips in the wire. Unless you're working with colored wire a lot, you can use your flat or round-nose pliers instead as long as you're careful. Check out the "Tackling Jobs with Pliers" section later in this chapter for info on these and other pliers.

✔ **Plastic coated wire** is base metal wire that's coated with brightly colored plastic. It looks similar to wire that you're used to. It bends easily, coils like a dream, and is perfect for kids. The bright colors available and the ease of use (and its relative low cost) make it a great choice for little hands and eyes.

✔ **Precious metal wire** is used for wire-wrapping, chain-making, and other jewelry. It's available in several metals (gold, platinum, gold-filled, and sterling silver), in three shapes (round, half-round, and square), and in three hardnesses (dead soft, half-hard, and full hard). Most jewelry makers stick with the gold-filled or sterling variety because they're more affordable, but still beautiful.

The more you bend precious metal wire, the more brittle it becomes, so be careful.

Like cord and thread, wire comes in several weights and widths, called *gauges*. As a rule, the higher the gauge, the thinner and softer the wire. So, 22-gauge is harder than 26-gauge. And 24- and 26-gauge dead soft round are ideal for a variety of projects, like the ones in Chapter 7 and Chapter 9 in particular. Keep a spool of these wires handy because they're easier to work with than some of the harder gauges.

Because precious metal prices fluctuate, prices for precious metal wire may also vary. Check out Chapter 7 for more details on wire sizes, hardness, and cool wire-wrapping techniques.

Getting the lowdown on metals lingo

At first, all the terminology surrounding metals, wire, and alloys, may seem overwhelming. Use this list to get up to speed:

✔ An *alloy* is a mix of metals. When a precious metal isn't pure, it's mixed with other substances to form an alloy.

✔ To *anodize* a metal means to create an oxidized coating on it. Often, colorful coatings are applied to metals like niobium and titanium to create beautifully colored metals for jump rings, other findings, and beads.

✔ The term *gold-filled* means that the items are made by mixing gold with another metal (usually a base metal like copper). Then the metal workers roll or *draw* the metal (pull it through a particular sized hole) to the desired diameter and shape. Gold-filled items are very durable. Allergic reactions to it are rare. Gold-filled metal is less expensive than pure gold, and it's commonly used by many jewelry makers for chains, earwires, and wire wrapping.

✔ *Gold-finished* and *silver-finished* items are sometimes called either *gold color* or *silver color* items. You may also hear the term *washed,* which means that the base metal is electroplated with a non-standardized thickness of gold, silver, or nickel. This option is less expensive than gold-filled items, but more expensive than gold-plated items, because the finished layer of precious metal is thicker than a plated layer.

✔ *Gold-plated, silver-plated,* and *nickel-plated* items have a very thin layer of precious metal applied, or *plated,* to the surface of the base metal. Because the plating is so thin, the plating can wear off after time. Plating is the least expensive and least durable option.

✔ *Karat (kt or k)* is the measure of purity of gold that's been used for centuries. In a nutshell, if an item is 24kt, it's 24 parts or 100 percent solid gold. Fourteen karat gold is 14 parts pure gold, and 10 parts other metal, for a total of 24 parts. Fourteen karats is the standard purity used for most jewelry, especially for wire and findings, which get a decent amount of wear and tear. Eighteen karat gold has a darker color with a deeper yellow tone and is much softer. It's often used for S-clasps that you bend to open and close.

✔ *Nickel silver* is an alloy of nickel, copper, and zinc. It contains no silver at all. Nickel silver looks a lot like sterling silver, but has a grayer tone. It's sometimes called German silver. It's durable and a great choice for jewelry making, especially when you're on a tight budget and aren't allergic to nickel.

✔ *Niobium* is used to strengthen alloys for industrial and commercial use, including high tech applications in the aerospace industry. The base metal itself is used extensively in jewelry making, because it's an inexpensive and hypoallergenic metal. After manufacturing into the desired shape, the naturally gray base metal niobium can be anodized to create colors.

✔ *Pewter* is an alloy traditionally made from tin, antimony, copper, and lead. It's a dull (as in not shiny), dark-silver-colored metal. It's used to fashion jewelry components as well as platters, drinking mugs, serving utensils, and other kitchen items. It's now available in a lead-free version. Some jewelry charms and pendants are cast in pewter, and then finished with a precious metal, or enameled to create a colorful finished piece.

(continued)

(continued)

✔ *Platinum* is the hardest and most valuable precious metal. It resembles white gold, but weighs significantly more. It retains its shine and needs little to no polishing. In the last 10 to 15 years, platinum exploded onto the fine jewelry market. Higher priced than gold, platinum findings, wires, and components aren't readily available.

✔ *Sterling silver* items are made of 92.5 percent pure silver and 7.5 percent copper or other metal. These proportions must be followed exactly or the item can't be called sterling silver. Sterling silver will tarnish over time and take on an antique look. If you'd prefer to keep your silver shiny, polish it with a silver jewelry cloth and keep its exposure to the air limited when you're not wearing it. If you display your sterling silver in a display case, purchase special anti-tarnish cloths to place in your cases to keep the tarnish to a minimum.

✔ *Surgical steel* is most often used in jewelry that pierces the skin, including earrings, belly rings, nose rings, and all other body jewelry. In some cases, just the *post*, the component that goes through the skin, is surgical steel and the rest may be base metal or an alloy. Surgical steel is hypoallergenic and safe for most people to wear. If you're extremely sensitive, look for nickel-free surgical steel.

✔ *Titanium* is one of the hottest metals in jewelry making today. It's a dark gunmetal gray and very lightweight. It's practically indestructible and won't take scratches and nicks. It's less expensive than platinum. When titanium oxidizes, it creates beautiful shades of yellow, pinks, and blues. Titanium is also used in medical implants, like screws, plates, and so on; it's hypoallergenic and tolerated by most people.

✔ A *troy ounce* is one of the main units of measurement in the weight system used for precious metals. Twelve troy ounces make up a troy pound. A troy ounce differs from a standard *avoirdupois* (the weight system used for food and non-precious metal items) ounce; one troy ounce weighs 31.1 grams while one avoirdupois ounce weighs 28.3 grams. So if you buy an ounce (that is, a troy ounce) of gold, you're getting more than a standard (avoirdupois) ounce of gold.

✔ *Vermeil* items are made of sterling silver, heavily electroplated with 22kt yellow gold.

Tackling Jobs with Pliers

While many projects can be done with your bare hands (like stringing and knotting), at some point you'll need jewelry pliers. Jewelry pliers are more delicate than the ones you'd find at a hardware store and have rubber tipped handles for more accurate gripping. They come in several shapes depending on your use. If at all possible, choose the ones with the built-in spring action for easier hold. It will save your hands and wrists.

Must-have pliers

These are the tools that I can't seem to get along without, using them in many projects. You can choose to buy them individually or in a set. Many online vendors and craft and bead stores, sell starter sets that include many (if not all) of these valuable tools all in one.

Here's the list of pliers that you want to have in your jewelbox:

- **Flat-nose pliers** have flat jaws and are for bending wire at angles, and to close jump rings. The flat smooth jaws hold round beads without nicking or scratching them. I also use mine to straighten wire that's bent or to hold a wire in place while I wrap wire around it. Check out Figure 2-1a to see what these look like.

- **Round-nose pliers** are used to make loops, all sizes of loops. The nose of the pliers are wide at the base and taper to smaller rounds. You wrap wire around the round nose to make loops. You can also use them to open and close jump rings. They're a must-have for wire wrapping or making long chains. If you can only buy one pair of pliers, this is the one to get. To take a look at these beauties, check out Figure 2-1b.

- **Wire cutters** are pliers used for cutting wire or cord. You can purchase these through a jewelry supply store or even at the hardware store. Definitely a good investment, you can find these in just about every size and shape. Find what works best for you. Figure 2-1c shows the basic variety.

Figure 2-1:
Must-have
pliers for
your
jewelbox.

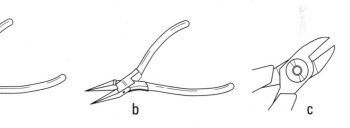

a   b   c

Nice additions to your jewelbox

Depending on what designs you want to tackle, you may need additional pliers. Many of the techniques that you perform with your must-have tools are simplified with these specialized tools. Because they are designed to do a specific job, they provide for a more professional-looking finished product.

Here's a list of common additions to specialty jewelboxes:

- **Bent-nose pliers** have a narrow tip that's bent in the shape of an "L." The bent nose helps you reach tough spots where ordinary pliers can't go. See them up close in Figure 2-2a.

- **Chain-nose pliers** come to a fine taper at the end and are used for gripping or bending angles in narrow areas. Extremely versatile, use these to pick up small beads and components, repair a finished piece, or anywhere else you need precision. Figure 2-2b shows you the details.

- While **crimp pliers** are not a requirement for using crimp beads (flat-nose or chain-nose pliers can be used to flatten the crimp bead down), the advantage of the crimp pliers is that the crimp bead, after being secured, is more rounded and cylindrical. The finished bead looks almost like a tube bead, instead of a smashed round bead. For more on working with crimp beads, take a look at the "Putting It Together: Choosing and Using Findings" section later in this chapter. See Figure 2-2c for a peek at this handy tool.

- **Loop-closing pliers** are grooved and smooth on the inside. Use them to close up loops, jump rings, bracelet links, and other connectors, without scratching the pieces and maintaining their original shape. Look at their round design in Figure 2-2d.

- **Long nose, or needle nose pliers** are similar to flat-nose pliers, but they have a longer tapered tip. See Figure 2-2e for the full picture.

- **Nylon jaw pliers** have replaceable nylon (rather than metal) jaws. They are designed to work with delicate articles and help you avoid scratching, chipping, and nicking the finish. They come in many different styles, so they can perform the same functions as loop-closing pliers, crimp pliers, stone-setting pliers, and so on, all without marring the finish of your pieces. Take a look at Figure 2-2f for a close up look.

- **Rosary pliers** are similar to round-nose pliers, but they also have a wire cutter at the joint where the two tips meet, for cutting wire or cord. At around $6, they make a great 2-in-1 tool. Use these for any job that requires you to quickly twist and cut wire. Figure 2-2g shows you the details.

- **Split-ring pliers** have a special tip designed to open split rings. If you work with split rings a lot, these can help save your wrists. (Personally, I just use my fingernail to pull them apart, but I don't use them very often.) See the "Connectors" section later in this chapter for more on working with split rings, and look at Figure 2-2h to see these pliers up close and personal.

- **Stone-setting pliers** are used to tighten prongs on rings, pendants, and earrings. These beauties are handy for working with vintage or estate jewelry finds. See Figure 2-2i to see how they work.

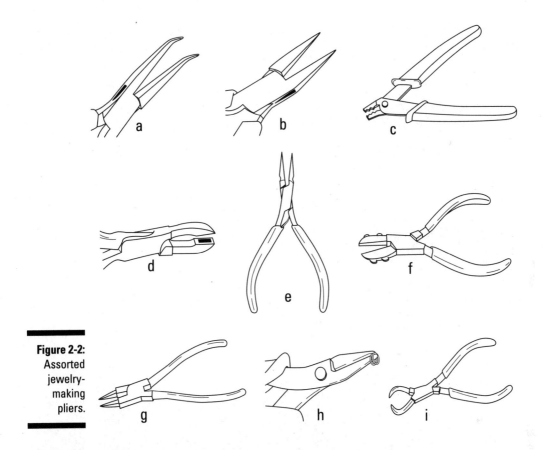

Figure 2-2:
Assorted
jewelry-
making
pliers.

Understanding the Importance of Measurements and Weights

Whether you're purchasing your beads and wire from a store, catalog, or
bead show, it's important to understand the terminology of the various measurement and weight standards so you know what you're buying. For example, when buying jewelry-making items in bulk, you usually buy beads and
crystals by the *gross,* or 144 objects (or 12 dozen). But you'll probably buy
pearls by the strand, which typically is 16 inches. Bead diameter is measured
in millimeters (mm), and wire gauge is measured in gauges, but its length is
measured in meters, yards, or feet. While you generally don't have to convert
everything to metric or standard measurements, I've included a few charts to
make life easier.

Check out Chapter 3 for information on how many beads make up a certain length strand. You can use the table to decide how many you need to make up your creation, or you can use it to see how many beads you get if you buy a particular strand.

When converting to or from metric units, look at the corresponding metric unit and its value for the specified imperial measurement units and/or U.S. customary units. With this information, shown in Table 2-1, you can do your own calculations for any precise metric conversion you need.

Table 2-1	Metric Conversions	
When You Know	*Multiply By*	*To Find*
Inches	25.4	Millimeters
Inches	2.54	Centimeters
Feet	30.5	Centimeters
Feet	0.305	Meters
Yards	0.914	Meters
Centimeters	0.394	Inches
Meters	1.09	Yards
Ounces	28.4	Grams
Pounds	454	Grams
Pounds	0.454	Kilograms
Grams	0.035	Ounces
Kilograms	2.20	Pounds

Putting It Together: Choosing and Using Findings

From headpins and eyepins to crimps and clasps to jump rings and split rings to earwires to posts to links and charms to bead caps and end caps, *findings* are the jewelry components that finish the design, keep it together, and make it unique. You can buy findings or make them yourself. In the following sections, I give you the details on what this stuff is. And in Chapter 7, I even show you how to make some of your own.

Connectors

Connectors are the components the help you connect the various parts of your jewelry pieces. They can hold beads in place, help you attach dangles, and connect earrings to your ears.

Headpins and eyepins

These are the ever-present jewelry components used to assemble earrings and dangles. Headpins come with either a flat, paddle-shaped, round base, or jeweled base. Headpins come in 14kt solid gold, gold-filled, sterling silver, silver-plated, copper, and niobium. Eyepins are very similar, except instead of the base, or *head,* they come with a small pre-made loop at one end, called an *eye.* Get a package of 10 each to start, in plated, sterling, or gold-filled. Figure 2-3 shows you the difference between a headpin and an eyepin.

For practice, though, you can by the cheaper version. If the package doesn't say "sterling," "gold-filled," or "plated," it's probably base metal.

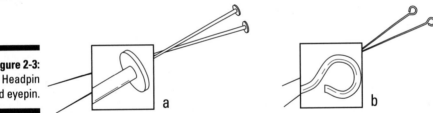

Figure 2-3:
Headpin
and eyepin.

a   b

Jump rings and split rings

Used by jewelry makers to connect clasps and pieces of jewelry together, jump rings and split rings are an important component in design. Jump rings require use of the pliers in order to be closed up, and they take practice so you don't over squeeze and break the jump ring. Split rings are fully closed and twist into place to connect two pieces together. Take a look at Figure 2-4a and b to see what a jump ring and a split ring look like, respectively.

Figure 2-4:
Jump ring
and split
ring.

a

b

Crimps

Ah crimps! Those soft-barrel hollow beads used to start and finish the ends of all beading wire, cord, leather, and thread — practice with crimp pliers and a few cheap plated crimps first and see what happens. Available mostly in sterling and plated silver or 14kt gold or gold-filled, some crimps come with an attached loop, some are smooth, and others are corrugated. Check out Figure 2-5 to see several examples of crimp beads.

Make sure to buy the right crimp size for your thread or cord. Buy crimp *tubes* for a stronger hold or a thicker strand; use crimp *beads* for a less strong hold, or a more delicate look. I like the 2x2mm and the 3x3mm crimp tubes, especially for multiple bead strands, but experiment to see which you prefer. You can even get micro-crimp pliers that work for smaller beads (1x1mm) and lighter weight wire (0.010).

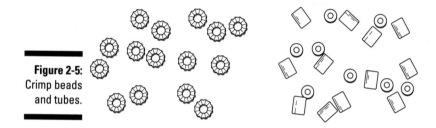

Figure 2-5: Crimp beads and tubes.

Earwires, posts, and clips

Also available in a variety of metals from silver to gold, from niobium to titanium, earwires are the standard for inserting a dangling earring into your ear. Posts are excellent for mounting half-drilled beads. Check out Figure 2-6 to view a smattering of earring finding options. The range of styles, weights, and shapes are mind boggling, including seashell and flower shapes, hoops, fish-hooks, and more — how do you choose?

Here are the key factors I consider when choosing which earwires are best for my projects:

✔ **Metal sensitivity:** If someone is allergic to plated silver, switch to niobium or gold. Many people (like my mom) can tolerate only hypoaller-genic earwires. It's useless to buy the cheapest thing, only to return it or never use it!

✔ **Price:** Earwires, posts, and clips vary from the dirt cheap (5¢ per pair) to very pricey ($30 per pair).

> ✔ **Sturdiness:** Some earring findings are made from thicker gauge wire that makes them sturdy but not as easy to work with, so consider the design and what shape and size you desire. Some shapes stay on the ear better; some get easily stuck in the wearer's hair or turtleneck sweater. You just have to check them out for yourself.

I prefer the sterling or 14kt gold-filled lever-back earwires because they're comfortable, rarely get snagged or tangled in hair or clothing, and stay in the ear, even with a night of salsa dancing. Try a few to see what works best for you.

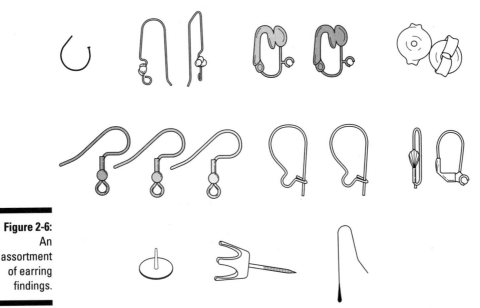

Figure 2-6:
An assortment of earring findings.

Clasps

A *clasp* is a special kind of jewelry finding that also you to put on and take off your piece of jewelry. There are hundreds, if not thousands, of clasps to choose from, in all kinds of metals and in all price ranges. Depending on your budget and design, here are a few of my favorites and some tips on buying.

Fishhook safety clasps

I prefer the safety feature and the filigree scrolled design of these clasps. The safety feature means that you have to pinch the tip to release it, and then unhook it. Some come with pre-made loops so you don't have to add jump rings, which makes life easier. In 18kt gold, they run about $10 each, silver ones are about $6 each; less in bulk. Take a look at Figure 2-7 to see what these clasps look like.

Figure 2-7:
Fishhook
safety
clasps.

Tube clasps

Sometimes called *slide clasps, tube clasps* are ideal for multi-strand pieces. They have pieces that slide into each other or snap in place. Available in several lengths and sizes, they are fun for chokers and thick beaded bracelets. Figure 2-8 shows you a tube clasp.

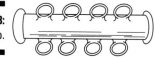

Figure 2-8:
Tube clasp.

Fancy clasps

Similar in filigree design to the fishhook clasps, *fancy clasps* come in round and box shapes but do not have the hook feature, because they only need to be squeezed to open. They still are a great deal and are very strong and pretty. Look for them in single or multi-strand designs as well. Stock up on a bunch of various shapes and sizes in either gold or silver. Check out Figure 2-9 to see a few examples of this design.

Figure 2-9:
Examples of
fancy
clasps.

Springring clasps

These are the round clasps you've probably seen on many traditional designs. They are used with a jump ring or a chain tab to complete the clasp and require pinching a release trigger that springs open and closed. These clasps are small and can be a bit tricky to see well. Take a look at Figure 2-10a and b to see a springring clasp and chain tab.

Figure 2-10:
Springring
clasp and
chain tab

Hook and eye and S clasps

While they do not have the pinch and hook safety feature, *hook and eye* and *S clasps* are better for older wearers who may not be able to use their fingertips as easily. The clasps are definitely strong, but they open more easily, so be careful, especially when bungee jumping or skydiving! Figure 2-11a and b show you the basic structure.

Figure 2-11:
Hook and
eye and S
clasps

a   b

Lobster claw clasps

Self-closing and streamlined, *lobster claws* are great for beaded jewelry and are easier to handle than the typical springring design. Pair these up with a jump ring, and you have a secure clasp. Take a look at Figure 2-12 for a close up.

Figure 2-12:
Lobster
claw clasp.

Toggle clasps

Extremely easy to open and close and ideal for necklaces and bracelets, *toggle clasps* are very popular and come in many styles and widths. Simply slip the pin or *toggle* through the center or *eye*. Cool designs are cropping up all the time, like a heart-shaped lock(eye) and key(pin). Figure 2-13 shows you examples of toggle clasps.

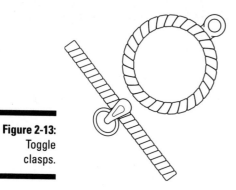

Figure 2-13:
Toggle
clasps.

Barrel and torpedo clasps

Available with pre-attached loops, *barrel* and *torpedo clasps* require twisting
to open and close, and the torpedo is simply a skinnier version of the barrel
shape. Either tie these clasps onto your thread or use a crimp bead to attach
them. See Figure 2-14a (barrel) and b (torpedo).

Figure 2-14:
Barrel and
torpedo
clasps.

a   b

Magnetic clasps

Magnetic clasps consists of two magnets attached to loops, a stroke of genius
if you hate dealing with all the twisting, screwing, pinching, and squeezing of
the other clasp options. While the magnetic clasps are rather strong, wear
them with care because they can pull apart under stress. See Figure 2-15.

Figure 2-15:
Magnetic
clasps.

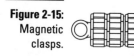

Bell clasps

Perfect for stringing multi-strand pieces or large beads, bell clasps are a neat
way to finish a design because the last bead is partially covered or hidden in

the open bell. The clasp mechanism is usually a hook and eye style, but they sport a fancy bell cap to cover up the last bead. See Figure 2-16.

Figure 2-16:
Bell clasps.

Connection to clasps: Clamshells, bead tips, and end caps

Used to conceal knots at the ends of beaded strands and to connect strands to clasps, clamshells, and bead tips are very useful little things. Usually, *bead tips* consist of a tiny cup with a hole on the bottom or side and a loop attached. *Clamshells* are commonly referred as the same thing as bead tips, and come in many styles, metals, and shapes. See Figure 2-17a and b.

End caps offer more variety, but their function is similar to bead caps, which hide the knot and end a strand, like the bell clasps. Some end caps can be used to terminate both beaded cord and thread and are available in either coiled or smooth versions with loops on the end. Some end caps can be pinched to secure the cord, or you can string the beading thread or wire through the end cap hole. See Figure 2-17c.

Figure 2-17:
Clamshells,
bead tips,
and end
caps.

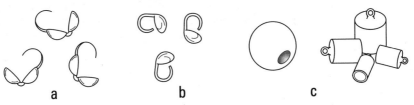

a   b   c

Project 2-1: Illusion Necklace

Illusion necklaces are widely popular necklaces that give the appearance that their beads are circling your neck without the aid of stringing material. They give the illusion that the stringing thread or cord is invisible. They can be created quickly, with just a few basic supplies. Take a look at Figure 2-20 for the finished project.

Tools and Materials

1 pair of flat-nose pliers

1 crimp pliers (optional, but recommended)

28 inches of clear thread, like Supplemax or Accuflex.

12 6mm round AB crystals, clear

26 2x2mm silver crimp beads

1 medium fishhook clasp in silver, with pre-attached loops

1. **Thread 1 crimp bead onto Supplemax.** Follow it with one end of the clasp, as shown in Figure 2-18a.

2. **Re-insert the thread back through both the clasp and the crimp.** See Figure 2-18b.

3. **Gently close crimp with crimp pliers, as shown in Figure 2-18c.**

4. **String 1 crimp bead through the other end of the thread.**

5. **Gently close the crimp and add 1 crystal.**

6. **Follow with another crimp bead. Gently crimp the second crimp bead to secure crystal in place.** Check out Figure 2-19 for details.

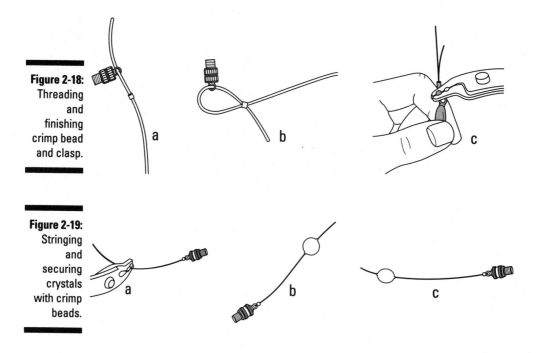

Figure 2-18: Threading and finishing crimp bead and clasp.

a   b   c

Figure 2-19: Stringing and securing crystals with crimp beads.

a   b   c

7. **Measure about 1 inch down the thread and add another crimp bead. Repeat Step 4 until you use all the crystals and all but one crimp bead.**

8. **String the last crimp bead and other end of clasp through thread.** Check out Figures 2-18a and b to see how it works.

9. **Close crimp with crimp pliers (refer to Figure 2-18c).**

10. **Connect the clasp and enjoy your finished project, as shown in Figure 2-20.**

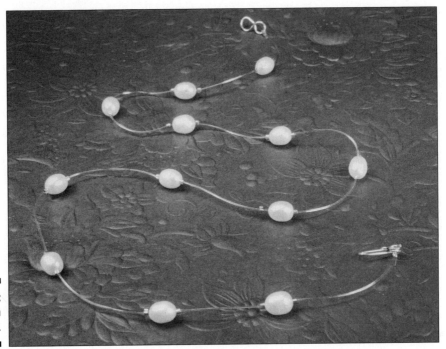

Figure 2-20:
Illusion
Necklace.

Cleaning it up

Often, a great first step when working with old jewelry is cleaning it up. Whether it's a cool charm bracelet you found at a flea market or an old brooch you discovered in your grandmother's jewelry box, clean it to see what you have to work with.

The number one rule is to start cautiously. You don't want to damage your piece. Be aware that vintage jewelry often has coatings or finishes that can be removed if you clean them too aggressively or use harsh chemicals. Decide whether you want that patina look to remain on your piece. If you do, don't use aggressive chemicals that could remove it.

Use caution when getting rhinestones wet. Moisture can move the foil backing that makes them sparkle if it has been previously damaged. It's not always obvious if the backing has been damaged so proceed with caution.

Here's my list (in order) of how to proceed with cleaning a vintage jewelry piece to do the least amount of damage:

- **Use a polishing cloth.** Technically, these polish (make brighter) rather than clean (remove dirt and grime), but it's a good first step to see what you're working with.

- **Spray jewelry cleaner on the piece.** Allow the cleaner to work for a bit, and then rub to remove dirt. I recommend spraying rather than immersing the piece because moisture may damage a piece (particularly rhinestones, pearls, or opals), and less is better until you know what you're working with.

- **Use a paste jewelry cleaner** if you know you're working with a precious metal that has no coating or patina that you want to keep. This is the step I take in Project 9-1 in Chapter 9. I was pretty sure that my piece was sterling silver, so I worked a little cleaner into the back of the piece to test it and confirm.

- **Use an ionic or sonic cleaner.** If you have one of these fancy machines, and feel like taking the plunge, immerse your find in this magical device.

Again, proceed with caution when using this or any cleaner with vintage jewelry because you never know what kind of life your piece may have had before finding it's way to you.

- **Consult a professional jeweler** about cleaning and restoring your piece. If you feel like you want to keep your piece intact, a professional may be a good stop on the road to recovery.

Chapter 3

Making Magic with Beads, Crystals, Pearls, and Stones

*I*n its most basic definition, a *bead* is anything that can be strung or threaded. So whether I'm talking about pearls, stones, crystals, or plastic, on some level, these are all materials that can be turned into beads. However, not all purists agree. Those who work with gemstone beads, in particular, often turn their noses up at plastic beads, because they prefer to work with beads made from natural materials.

Beads are usually the most important and costly items you need in making your jewelry. However, given the vast array of beads available, including a variety of pearls, stones, and crystals from around the world, choosing what to buy is probably the hardest part of your entire design process!

In this chapter, I identify many of the beads, stones, and pearls available. I show you where to find them and how to get the most from their beauty and at the greatest value. I also give you the details on semi-precious stones and their fabled healing properties. Finally, you get to play around with various bead textures, colors, and shape for a truly unique look — and one that may have the power to make you feel good, too.

Bead Basics

Whether you shop online or in a physical store, you'll find an endless range of beads, from leaves, hearts, and other shapes to shell beads and simulated gem strands to lampwork, cat's eye, dichroic, Italian glass, metal beads, and more. Choose beads that appeal to you based on their shape, size, color, or shimmer. The great thing about beaded jewelry is that if you put it together and don't like how it looks, you can tear your piece apart and rework it. Experiment until you find combinations that work for you.

Identifying man-made beads

Here are descriptions for some of my favorite beads and favorite ways to use them to help you decide what's best for your design.

- ✔ **Dichroic glass beads:** *Dichroic* glass literally means multi-colored glass. It's created by fusing layers of glass together in a vacuum and simultaneously depositing metal oxides in the glass. When you look at a bead, pendant, or other jewelry component made from dichroic glass, you can see many layers, textures, and colors, despite the smooth surface. These beads are very shiny, vibrant, and are an excellent choice for a pendant or central bead in your design.

- ✔ **Cat's eye beads:** You can recognize cat's eye beads by their signature band of color in the middle of the bead. They usually contrast two colors (like red and orange or purple and white) in a dramatic fade from one to the other and back again. Their shimmering, dual luster creates a dramatic "eye" in the center of the bead, reminiscent of the eye of a cat. They pair well with metal spacers, stones, or pearls. Choose colors to complement a particular outfit or occasion for a customized look. These beads are available either in their natural state (carved from quartz) or man-made from glass.

- ✔ **Czech glass beads:** Sometimes called *Czech* (pronounced "check") *pressed* glass, this type of bead is available in just about any shape imaginable. Rather than being heated and shaped by hand, it's heated and pressed into molds. In the lower quality beads, you actually see a seam in the middle of the bead. Incidentally, you can find other styles of Czech beads including *druk beads,* perfectly round beads in every size and color, and Czech fire-polished beads, which have a high shine. Some Czech beads sport a hand-painted design, like flowers or dots reminiscent of lampwork beads. You can always add these where you need a little glitter here and there.

- ✔ **Lampwork beads:** Artists create these beads by heating glass canes with a torch, and then wrapping the melting glass around a rod, called a *mandrel,* to shape it. The finished beads are *annealed,* subjected to high heat and then slowly cooled, in glass *kilns,* specialized ovens, to improve their durability and strength. Lampwork beads, shown in Figure 3-1, often have swirling or raised designs in metallic or coordinating colors applied after the initial bead is formed, giving them a bumpy appearance. They are handmade and extremely popular for everything from earrings to necklaces and bracelets.

✔ **Metal beads:** Metal beads are highly versatile. You can find any shape and style bead made from metal. Metal beads are made from pewter, brass, gold, sterling silver, gold or silver plate, *vermeil* (sterling silver electroplated with 22kt gold), and other base metals. There is no limit to the designs, styles, and combinations available in metal beads. Many metal beads come in simple, smooth, polished forms. Others, like Bali beads, are highly detailed with intricate shapes. You can find metal beads inlaid with precious and semi-precious stones that serve as excellent focal points for any design. Or use smaller rounds, saucer-shaped, or flower-shaped beads as spacers to complement larger beads of any shape. The price of metal beads varies by the type of metal used to create them and the time that goes into their creation. Handmade beads are more expensive than the machine-made version and are sometimes priced depending on their gram weight.

✔ **Cloisonné:** Skilled artisans create each cloisonné piece using enameling techniques. They solder tiny tracts of precious metals onto the base bead to create a frame for the design, and then meticulously fill the frames with enameling powder and fire the pieces again and again after each application to melt the powder and create the gorgeous designs. Finally, they are highly polished to reveal the final design. See Figure 3-2. Using a cloisonné bead gives any design an Asian feel. They make great choices for pendants or accents within a larger piece.

✔ **Spacer beads:** Spacer beads are a key element in any design. They can be made out of just about anything, but they all share a common quality: They give your eye a break and let other beads take center stage. Their purpose is to separate or space out the core design elements. Without the break that spacer beads provide, you couldn't appreciate the complete shape, design, or surface of the components. Almost anything can be used as a spacer bead, but typical spacer shapes include small round beads, doughnuts, flat flower, and tiny tubes. Some spacers, like doughnuts, have a much larger stringing hole than other beads. Because they're intended to be used between larger beads, don't worry that they'll slip off. Check out Figure 3-3 for examples of several spacer bead styles.

✔ **Seed beads:** Seed beads are tiny beads used for looming, weaving, embellishing, and much more. They come in a range of sizes from tiny to extra super tiny. (Okay, not the technical names, but they are really small.) They are so small, in fact, that to string them, you definitely want to use a needle. The smallest are called Delica seed beads, which have a huge variety of colors, transparencies, and finishes. Sometimes the stringing hole is lined with a different color, giving the bead a different look. You can also find square, triangle, teardrop, and hex-cut seed beads that can add a little more sparkle to your design.

Fire Mountain Gems and Beads™ (www.firemountaingems.com/fordummies)

Figure 3-1:
Lampwork
beads.

Fire Mountain Gems and Beads™ (www.firemountaingems.com/fordummies)

Figure 3-2:
Cloisonné
beads.

The higher the seed bead size number, the smaller it is. So the 11/0 seed beads are larger than the 15/0.

Seed beads are sold by weight. For example, a 7.5-gram container of Delica seed beads contains approximately 1,600 beads and costs about $2. A 50-gram pouch has roughly 10,500 to 11,000 beads and costs in the neighborhood of $8.

Figure 3-3:
Several
spacer bead
examples.

Fire Mountain Gems and Beads™ (www.firemountaingems.com/fordummies)

Getting familiar with bead shapes

Many beads are cut into shapes. The shape of the beads you choose adds as much to the beauty of your work as the color or type of material you select. While you can find most of these bead shapes for most semi-precious stones, crystals, glass, and other mediums, most *faceted styles,* or styles with flat polished cuts added to them, were traditionally reserved for glass and crystal beads. Facets are added to stones to increase shine and sparkle. But facets can be added to any stone. In fact, even pearls are available today as faceted beads.

Here are some descriptions of some common bead shapes. Check out Figure 3-4 to see the shapes in living color (well, actually in black and white).

- ✔ **Round:** As the name implies, this bead is shaped like a sphere and round all over.

- ✔ **Teardrop:** A *teardrop bead* has one narrow pointed end, while the other is wider and rounded. Teardrops can be flat or rounded on their front and back faces. The hole for teardrop beads is either down through the center (lengthwise) or through the side near the top, referred to as *side-drilled* or *pendant-drilled.*

- ✔ **Oval:** Oval beads are rounded beads that are narrow on the ends and wider in the middle. Look for flat ovals and rounded ovals. When looking at pearls, the ovals are often called rice-shaped.

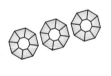
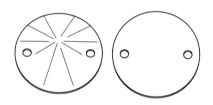

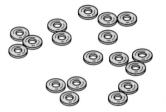
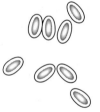

Figure 3-4:
Some
common
bead
shapes.

- ✔ **Doughnut:** Sometimes called rings, *doughnuts* are round, flat, and have a large hole in the middle. This hole can be used as the stringing or threading hole, but often doughnuts are connected together with jump rings or wire so that they lie flat against the skin. Some doughnuts also have edge-to-edge holes so they can be strung and lay flat against the skin.

- ✔ **Tube:** *Tubes* can be long, short or anywhere in between. They are always longer than they are wide and are fairly narrow. Use them as spacers between beads of other shapes for interesting contrast.

- ✔ **Rondelle:** *Rondelles* are kind of like squished round beads. They are flatter than round beads and are often, but not always, faceted. The facets add significant sparkle to an otherwise ordinary bead. Rondelle is the number-one selling crystal shape. Pair them with bicone beads, cubes, or tubes for non-stop sparkle.

- ✔ **Bicone:** *Bicone beads* are shaped like two cones stacked base to base. Both ends are narrow, while the center is wider. They are available in smooth or faceted styles.

- ✔ **Briolette:** *Briolette* is the fancy name for a faceted, rounded, teardrop-shaped bead. Some people call it a *drop bead*. These are most often side-drilled.

- ✔ **Cabochon:** A *cabochon,* sometimes shortened to just *cab,* is flat on one side, but that flat side isn't seen when the piece is worn. Instead, the flat side is affixed to a backing or wrapped in wire. Cabochons can be large or small and worn as pendants, used as dangles, attached to links of a bracelet, or used any many other ways.

- ✔ **Cube:** *Cubes* are great all-purpose beads. They are square-shaped and fully 3-D. Each of their six sides is the same size. Look for cubes with letters for fun name bracelets. You can also find crystal cubes that are hand-faceted. Most semi-precious stones come in cubes and look cool paired with crystals, in earrings, necklaces, or bracelets.

- ✔ **Lentil:** A *lentil* is a rounded bead that's flat on one side, just like split lentil that you make into soup. Crystal lentils are usually highly faceted, much like a rondelle on the rounded side. Choose them for projects like bracelets or necklaces that lay flat against the skin rather than items like earrings that dangle freely.

- ✔ **Half-back:** *Half-back beads* are basically half of a bicone bead. These beads are similar to lentils because they're flat on the back, but instead of being drilled from edge to edge, they are drilled from the top down.

All beads can be drilled horizontally (edge to edge) or vertically (top to bottom). Check out Figure 3-5 to see the difference. Both orientations can be useful depending on your particular design. Vertically drilled beads are often used for earrings or stringing on a necklace. But if you're interested in creating a statement with a large center bead or a pendant, consider choosing a horizontally (also referred to as side-drilled) drilled bead instead.

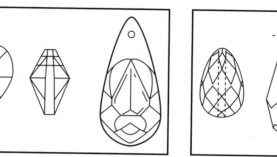

Figure 3-5: Example of vertically and horizontally drilled beads.

Understanding bead sizes

Beads come in many different sizes, most often measured in millimeters (the abbreviation for millimeters is *mm*). One inch is equivalent to about 25 millimeters. Check out Table 3-1 to find out how many beads you need to create your designs.

All the numbers in Table 3-1 are approximate. If your beads aren't all the same size, the number you need varies.

Table 3-1	Approximate Number of Beads Needed for Specific Lengths of Beaded Strands									
Bead Size	*Length of Beaded Strand*									
	6"	*8"*	*10"*	*12"*	*14"*	*16"*	*20"*	*24"*	*28"*	*32"*
3mm	51	68	85	102	119	136	170	204	238	271
4mm	39	51	64	77	89	102	127	153	178	204
6mm	26	34	43	51	60	68	85	102	119	136
8mm	20	26	32	39	45	51	64	77	89	102
10mm	16	21	26	31	36	41	51	61	72	82
12mm	13	17	22	26	30	34	43	51	60	68
14mm	11	15	19	22	26	29	37	44	51	59
16mm	10	13	16	20	23	26	32	39	45	51
18mm	9	12	15	17	20	23	29	34	40	46

When you're working with larger beads, allow more room on your thread or wire for the finished piece if it will be worn close to the skin, in for example, a choker or bracelet design. A bead's hole is often drilled in the middle of the bead, which means that a large bead offers more space between the thread going through the hold and the your skin. For smaller beads, give yourself a little extra space. Measure the interior diameter of the necklace rather than the length of the necklace to make sure your piece will fit you. Take a look at Figure 3-6 to see how big an individual bead is.

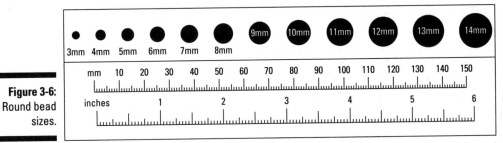

Figure 3-6: Round bead sizes.

Fire Mountain Gems and Beads™ (www.firemountaingems.com/fordummies)

Using Crystals

Crystal is simply glass infused with a small amount of lead. The chemicals (generally metal oxides) used during the heating process (rather than dyes), determine the color of the crystal. Different chemicals absorb different wavelengths of visible light. And the human eye sees the opposite of the absorbed color. For example, if the chemical added absorbs red, you see a green crystal. Because a clear, colorless crystal contains no impurities, it's tougher to make one than its colorful cousins. Even minor contamination introduced during the manufacturing process could change the clarity of the crystal.

Because the lead is stabilized in the glass, crystals aren't toxic. But because they can shatter if crushed or damaged and the resulting pieces are very small and sharp, crystals should not be stored near children or pets. If children work with crystals, they should do so only with adult supervision.

Crystal beads come in numerous shapes, cuts, and sizes and are sold in packages of loose beads. You can also find individual crystals at any bead store. Their popularity has exploded recently because their colors range from topaz to sapphire. They are truly versatile design elements and can be used with anything including pearls, stones, and metals. They come with finishes, the most common being *AB*, which stands for *Aurora Borealis*, an iridescent clear coat that adds sparkle to a clear or flat color. One of my favorite shapes is the faceted bicone shape because it can be mixed with round beads for tremendous sparkle. Whether glued, strung on thread, set or wrapped in metal, you can use crystals in a variety of ways.

Designing crystal jewelry

Combine various styles and shapes of beads, like rondelles and half-back beads, to create an interesting look, or use them as end caps for an elegant touch. Let your creativity be your guide to create your own accessories, gifts for friends, or even merchandise to sell. Make the glamorous, but simple, Crystal Drop Earrings to try your hand at choosing and using crystals.

Project 3-1: Crystal Drop Earrings

Inspired by old Hollywood, drop (sometimes called dangle) earrings have been an evening fashion staple spanning several decades. Maybe it's because their length makes your neck appear longer and the crystals make your face appear brighter. Choose any type or size stone, or crystal, based on your preference and your budget. For simplicity, I use the basic clear crystal teardrop with an AB (stands for Aurora Borealis, which means an iridescent) finish. Check out Figure 3-8 for a peek at the finished project.

Tools and Materials

1 round-nose pliers

1 flat-nose pliers

1 wire cutter

2 1½-inch-long plain or jeweled sterling silver headpins (wires with a flat head on one end)

2 4-inch long sterling silver eyepins (wires with a tiny loop on one end)

2 sterling silver leverback hinged earwires (I prefer these, because the

earring becomes a bit heavy with all the dazzling crystals, the leverback is a safer bet. If you prefer kidney-shaped or fishhook earwires, or even clip-ons, go for it.)

2 15x10mm crystal AB teardrops with a vertically drilled hole (refer to Figure 3-5)

20–26 6mm diamond-shaped or bicone crystal beads in any color.

1. **Stack 10 to 13 bicone beads on one silver eyepin.** I used 13 beads in each of my earrings because I wanted to go for the maximum sparkle to impress the celebs at the awards ceremony.

   The more beads you use, the longer your earrings will be. You could use fewer than what's called for if you have a shorter eyepin. A 2-inch eyepin, for example, holds about 8, so for 2 earrings, you'd need 16 beads in all.)

2. **On the straight end of the eyepin, take your round-nose pliers and gently form a small, open loop, while holding the beaded eyepin in your other hand.** Don't fully close the loop yet, because you'll need to connect it to the loop at the bottom of your earwire. Take a look at Figure 3-7a to see how this works.

3. **Connect one earwire to the open loop you've just made with your eyepin.** Figure 3-7b shows you how. Secure the loop closed with your flat-nose pliers. See Figure 3-7c.

   Be gentle! When closing the "eye" of your eyepin, don't squeeze the handle of your pliers too much or your "eye" will flatten and no longer be round in shape.

4. **Slide the teardrop crystal onto a headpin. Trim any excess wire with the wire cutters, leaving about ¼ inch of wire extending beyond the crystal. Form a small, open loop at the top with the remaining ¼ inch with your round-nose pliers.**

5. **Connect the open loop of your headpin to the bottom loop on your eyepin.** Secure the loop closed (but not too tight) with your flat-nose pliers.

6. **Repeat for other earring.** Make sure you use the same number of bicone beads on this earring that you chose in the first one, so they're the same length.

7. **Hold earrings up to face, smile, and prepare your Oscar acceptance speech.**

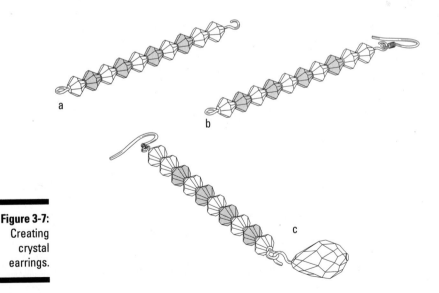

Figure 3-7:
Creating
crystal
earrings.

Figure 3-8:
Crystal Drop
Earrings.

I suggest using Austrian made crystals by Swarovski, because they're the finest quality and provide the biggest bang for your buck. But if you're looking to trim down your bead budget a bit, look for Czech crystals, which are nearly as nice and a bit cheaper. Check out Chapter 15 for great places to get Swarovski crystals and other jewelry-making supplies. In fact, I have a customer that had a tight budget for her bridal jewelry. I used Swarovski crystals for the focal point teardrops, but mixed Czech crystals and fresh water pearls for the bulk of the beadwork. This blending brought the price down quite a bit and still gave her a stunning necklace for her wedding.

Selecting the best crystals for your budget

While several glass and crystal bead brands exist, Swarovski Austrian crystals are considered the finest products of their kind because of their wide spectrum of colors, unbeatable quality, and precise cut. That said, a package of 100 6mm bicone crystal beads sets you back about $20, and a package of 4mm bicone crystal beads runs you about $12. I think the quality is well worth the extra few bucks. Of course, if you're buying in large quantities, you can get that price down. I'm just giving you the high end of what to expect to pay in small quantities so you won't be shocked at the checkout counter. If you try these beauties and love them, start shopping for the best prices. Create a table like Table 3-2 to help you organize your pricing comparisons. I've included a couple examples to get you started.

Table 3-2		Comparing Crystal Prices		
Type of Crystal	*Quantity*	*Vendor*	*Price*	*Comments*
6mm bicone AB	144	ABC Beads	$27.50	Free shipping
6mm bicone AB	100	XYZ Supplies	$21.95	
6mm bicone AB	10	Mom & Pop's Shop	$4	Closed Sunday

The round and bicone shape are the most popular and widely available crystals, but you can find crystals in a host of other shapes, including heart shaped, doughnut or ring shaped, teardrop, and cubes. Older cuts, colors, and patterns are often discontinued as other newer shapes and cuts are created. If you find one that's unusual and you really like it or use it often, stock up, because it may not be around for long.

Sometimes a store sells the last batch of antique-look crystals. Antique can mean that the beads are very old, or it can mean that the style has been discontinued, making them collectible. Get the full story from your seller so you know which you're getting.

Cracking the crystal code

The name of the color for each Swarovski crystal represents the basic crystal color and the coating applied to the crystal, if there is one. By basic crystal color, I mean the color of the glass itself. The coating is a surface finish that is applied to the glass to enhance its appearance.

When the basic color of the glass is clear and colorless, the name of the color starts with the word *Crystal.* Take the popular bead color called Crystal AB for example. It starts with the word *Crystal* because it's made from clear, colorless glass, followed by *AB* for the *Aurora Borealis* coating. The AB coating gives crystals the iridescent rainbow appearance.

Many colors are then followed up with the shape of the bead to identify the name of the exact bead you're looking at. So the *Crystal AB bicone* is a clear crystal with an Aurora Borealis coating shaped like a bicone, or diamond.

Who doesn't want a piece of jewelry custom-made for them? Maybe you're not ready to bend someone's name in wire and mount it on a necklace, but you can whip up a quick pair of earrings featuring your best friend's birthstone. Use Table 3-3 to customize jewelry by matching the color of crystals to specific birthstones. Often the name of the color is the same as the name of the genuine gemstone, making it pretty easy!

Table 3-3	Getting Creative with Birthstones	
Month	*Stone*	*Crystal Alternative (Stone Color)*
January	Garnet, rose quartz	Siam, garnet, or rose (deep to light red)
February	Amethyst, onyx	Amethyst or jet (light purple or black)
March	Aquamarine, red jasper	Aquamarine (very pale blue)
April	Diamond, rock crystal	Crystal AB (clear)
May	Emerald, chrysoprase	Emerald (dark green)
June	Moonstone, pearl	Light topaz, smoky topaz, (light tan or pearl)
July	Ruby, carnelian	Siam or garnet (rich deep red)
August	Peridot, aventurine	Peridot (light green)
September	Sapphire, lapis lazuli	Sapphire or Montana sapphire (dark blue)
October	Tourmaline, opal	Smoky topaz (dark tan-purple)
November	Citrine, topaz	Topaz or Colorado topaz (tan)
December	Zircon, turquoise	Light sapphire or topaz (light blue or orange-red)

Rather than buying a few packs of different-colored crystals, consider buying a single large assorted pack. You can experiment with different combinations of colors and finishes, plus you generally get a better price per bead. Assortments are a great way to get started using any new product.

Wisdom on Pearls

Pearls are no longer a jewelry accessory you store in a box waiting for your next wedding invitation. And they're no longer available in only a few select strand lengths, with few pearl sizes. They have definitely come into their own. They run the gamut in terms of color, size, and shape. They're hot, trendy, and classic all at the same time.

Because the price has been dropping for the last several years, you don't need to wait to inherit some from your great aunt's third cousin. With the current supply of freshwater pearls, it's entirely possible that you could afford some of your very own right now. And even if you can't buy the genuine article now, you can use excellent glass faux pearls in many of your designs.

The pearl is unique because it's the only gem grown inside a living organism. Technically, they're organic gems rather than gemstones, because they come from living organisms. Natural pearls are formed when an irritant — a piece of shell, a scale, or a grain of sand becomes lodged inside a mollusk. The irritant becomes the pearl's nucleus, or center, as it's coated over several years with layers of *nacre,* or lustrous outer shell, inside the oyster. The size and shape of the nucleus and the region of the ocean where the mollusk lives all affect the final size, color, and shape of the pearl.

Natural pearls are pearls that are made without any interference from people. They are extremely rare and expensive, because overfishing and pollution plague the beds known for producing natural pearls. Instead most pearls are *cultured,* or helped along by people. Check out the "Cultured pearls" section later in this chapter for the full story.

Never use jewelry polish meant for stones or silver to clean your genuine pearls. Pearls are too porous and may decompose or peel. Instead, simply use a little liquid soap and water. Treat your pearls with care, and they should last a lifetime. The natural oils in your skin may change the color of the pearls over a long period of time, but that only adds to their luster and beauty.

Table 3-4	Pearl Pricing for Round Pearls		
Type of Pearl	*Size of Bead*	*Quantity*	*Prices*
Faux	6–7mm	16-inch strand	$1.50 and up
Cultured freshwater	6–7mm	16-inch strand	$15 and up
Cultured saltwater	6–7mm	16-inch strand	$185 and up

Natural pearls vary greatly in price, depending on their shape, size, and color. Refer to Table 3-2 for an example. A 6–7mm semi-round freshwater pearl with a decent off-white luster runs about $15 a strand, but don't expect every pearl to be exactly the same size and shape. That's the beauty of nature — it's not supposed to be perfect. If you want perfect, be prepared to pay for it.

Check out the Gemological Institute of America (www.gia.org) for information about pearls and other gemstones.

Faux pearls

To save your self some trial and error, start with a package of faux glass, rather than plastic pearls found at any crafts store. Glass pearls are only slightly more expensive than plastic, but the jewelry you create with them is heavier and more professional looking. They come in many sizes, shapes, and colors. While pink, ivory, and white glass pearls are widely available, you may also look for glass pearls with a metallic finish or ones with facets, depending on your taste. Glass pearls come in sizes similar to that of freshwater and cultured pearls. Refer to Figure 3-6 for common round bead sizes. Their care and cleaning is pretty much the same as natural pearls, but don't expect faux pearls to last forever. They're simply glass beads with a pearlized coating, so over time, the coating will start to peel. For beginning jewelry-making purposes, machine-made faux pearls are often easier to work with, because their sizes and holes are so uniform. Refer to Table 3-4 for information on prices for faux (or any other kind of) pearls.

If you run a strand of pearls across your teeth, genuine pearls have a sandy or grainy feel. Faux pearls are smooth.

Cultured pearls

In pearl lingo, the word "culture" has nothing to do with class, refinement, or yogurt with acidophilus. It simply means that pearl farmers have helped the process along by inserting an irritant into the shell of the oyster or mussel. The animal then secretes the nacre that forms around the irritant, creating the pearl. Naturally occurring pearls are extremely rare, due to overfishing and pollution. Instead, most pearls are cultured and raised in farms where they are nurtured and protected.

Freshwater pearls grow in mussels, while saltwater pearls grow in oysters. Typically, the shape difference of the shell itself has accounted for shape differences between the two types of pearls. However, Chinese farmers are increasingly producing round freshwater cultured pearls in huge numbers, driving down the cost.

You may notice that some of the holes of the pearls are very small, so purchase a *bead reamer,* a tool designed to slightly and gently increase the diameter of a bead's hole, just in case you get a few pearls that won't fit through your thread or wire.

Two main types of pearls are sold today: cultured saltwater pearls and cultured freshwater pearls. Don't let the word "cultured" fool you into thinking that they are something extra special. (Of course pearls are special, but I mean, special by pearl standards.) Some natural pearls are harvested today, but most freshwater and saltwater pearls are cultured. Catalogs and printed advertisements, in particular, like to use the word *cultured,* perhaps to imply a higher value.

You'll notice a substantial price difference between saltwater and freshwater pearls. Saltwater pearls are much more costly to produce for a few reasons. Oysters produce one or two saltwater pearls each. Freshwater mussels are producing as many as 40 to 50 pearls each. The freshwater beds are much easier to keep uncontaminated and unpolluted than saltwater beds as well, practically ensuring a larger harvest than their saltwater cousins.

As a rule, the richer the luster and more perfectly round (or less bumpy the shape), the more expensive the pearl.

No internationally recognized standard exists for grading pearls. But you may see or hear pearls described as A, AA, or AAA pearls. Because there's no consistency in the grading, one company's AA pearl is another company's A pearl. For the most part, using letters like A or AA are marketing descriptions and don't accurately describe pearl quality.

Here's a list of considerations when selecting pearls for jewelry making:

✔ **Color:** The traditional pearl is white. But it's not typical for pearls to be white straight from the mollusk. In most cases for the standard white pearl, the gems have been bleached, usually with light. Pink, lilac, and peach are all naturally occurring colors for pearls. In addition to the overall color of the pearl, they sometimes have an overtone color. White pearls, for example, often have a slight pink or slight green tint. Even black pearls can have an overtone.

✔ **Orient:** Orient describes whether or not the pearl has an iridescent quality or appearance. The pearl's orient allows the pearl to appear to change colors slightly as the light hits it.

✔ **Luster:** Luster describes the pearl's shine or sparkle. The higher the luster, the sharper the reflection you'll see in the pearls surface.

✔ **Size:** Size is probably the most objective attribute. You can easily measure a pearl and determine its size, refer to Figure 3-6 to see actual bead sizes. As a range, 3mm pearls are fairly small and 8mm pearls are fairly large. Anything over 8mm is extremely large and rare.

✔ **Shape:** The round shape is the most recognizable pearl shape, and is still the most popular. But don't overlook the amazing variety of shapes in your jewelry designs. Check out Figure 3-9 for a peek at the differences in pearl shapes.

- Potato: Semi-round, symmetrical

- Rice: Oval shaped, symmetrical

- Button: Round on one side, but squished flat on the opposite side, symmetrical

- Teardrop: Symmetrically aligned from side to side, but more narrow and pointed on one end, and wider and rounder on the other

- Stick: Pointed, somewhat jagged, non-symmetrical

- Baroque: Irregularly shaped, non-symmetrical

The *symmetry* of the shape of the pearl is incredibly important to its value. If a pearl has symmetry it means if you draw a line down the middle of the pearl, both sides look the same.

✔ **Surface quality:** The smoother and more blemish-free the surface of a pearl, the higher the value. A *blemish* is a little dent or mark on the surface of the pearl. Pearl surface quality can range from smooth to heavily blemished.

✔ **Nacre:** The pearl's *nacre* is the coating secreted by the mollusk around the irritant to create the pearl. The thicker the nacre, the higher the price of the pearl. Because some pearls are cultured by placing a bead in the mollusk as an irritant, the nacre may be thin even if the pearl itself is big. It can be a problem, because a thin nacre can chip much more easily than a thick one, greatly diminishing the appearance of the pearl over time.

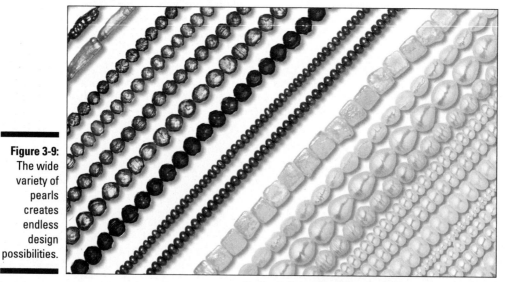

Figure 3-9:
The wide variety of pearls creates endless design possibilities.

Fire Mountain Gems and Beads™ (www.firemountaingems.com/fordummies)

White Lotus™ *Deep Lustre Cultured Freshwater Pearls*

Buy what you like. So much of the criteria used to price pearls are truly subjective, so your opinion definitely matters.

Working with Stones

What would-be-princess or wanna-be pirate hasn't pictured a treasure box overflowing with gems and gold pieces? Maybe that dream can't actually come true for most of us, but you can create a little piece of that fantasy for yourself by crafting jewelry from gems and stones.

Identifying stones and gems

While there are thousands of stones and gems, many with similar names and colors, I've tried to list some of the most popular ones here. As you visit bead stores or go to bead shows, you keep discovering new stones. In fact there are entire books and catalogs that focus on describing different stones.

Here's the list of fairly common gems and stones you should be able to find at your local bead store or online bead vendor.

- **Agate:** Agate is a semi-opaque stone, available in many different colors including, blues, greens, yellow, pinks, and black. Agate typically has stripes of color variations or blends that make it an interesting addition to any jewelry piece. Its mixture of vibrant colors blends well with pink and white pearls.

  If blue is your color, *blue agate* is a must-have for you. In its natural form, this agate is often gray. If you're creating jewelry that resembles the water or sky, try combining this semi-translucent stone with a variety of other blue beads — like various shapes and shades of Austrian crystals. Enhance it by mixing it with other cool colors such as greens and lavenders. Blue agate is often used to create *Intaglia cameos,* or cameos carved from the back that have a smooth top.

- **Amazonite:** For cool and calm, think amazonite. These blue-green beads add a sense of tranquility to all your jewelry. For a distinctive look, try it with black onyx or combine it with red-streaked green and white bloodstone or green and blue crystals.

- **Amber:** A semi-transparent yellow-gold soft stone, amber gives off a delicate, sweet smell when rubbed or warmed. In fact, it can actually burn, because it's fossilized tree resin. It has been used in medicines, jewelry, and religious artifacts for thousands of years. Use it to warm up any design from teardrop earrings to a choker. Mix with onyx or carnelian for a taste of fall anytime.

✔ **Amethyst:** The most popular quartz is probably amethyst. It ranges from a light lilac to a deep purple, the color of royalty. It's a rich and popular multipurpose gemstone. Most people think of it as a stone with exceptional spiritual power. This highly valued and most popular quartz works well in pendants and earrings or in a strand of beads or briolettes. Faceted amethyst with tiny pearls is also a beautiful combination.

✔ **Ametrine:** A delicate blend of quartz containing both amethyst and citrine, ametrine is beautiful. It's a newer gemstone, discovered less than 30 years ago. Depending how the gem is cut, you can have either more purple with a splash of yellow or vice versa. Choose beads for what appeals to you, and you can't go wrong.

✔ **Apatite:** It's usually bright sea green, but can also be found in yellows, blues, browns, and purples. Its name means "to deceive," because many early merchants mistook it for more valuable stones like peridot. It's used less often in jewelry making, because it's not as hard as other stones. Use it carefully in pieces that won't receive daily wear.

✔ **Aquamarine:** Sparkling, light blue to blue-green aquamarine is a strong stone. Few are actually mined and found naturally in their signature color. Instead, paler, duller stones are heated until the desired color is reached, or they are dyed though the dyed forms may be somewhat brittle. Use it in rings, pendants, or exquisite ankle bracelets.

✔ **Aventurine:** Because aventurine is a hard stone, it is popular with stone carvers and, therefore, is an excellent resource for beads, cabochons, and other types of decorative components. The colors range from light to medium green, although some forms of aventurine are also available in reds, blues, grays, and oranges. It contains small flecks of mineral inclusions giving it extra sparkle. A poor-man's jade, green aventurine has a look similar to jade without the cost.

✔ **Black onyx:** The natural color of onyx is a creamy mixture of beige, brown, and off-white. For beads, it is seldom sold in its natural state and instead is generally dyed black. This is a great stone for making men's jewelry, and it also looks wonderful with sterling silver.

✔ **Blue topaz:** Assigned as a birthstone to November or December, depending on whom you ask, blue topaz is a form of quartz and comes in light to medium shades of blue. It is a favorite of fine jewelers who include it in high-end gold jewelry, most often as a faceted set stone. But you can also find blue topaz beads for your own designs. One word of warning, however: Because these stones are often color treated, don't leave dyed quartz in bright light or it will fade.

✔ **Carnelian:** Like many gemstones, carnelian is normally treated to darken its color, which ranges from light orange to dark burgundy. The darker the stone, the more you can bet it's been color enhanced. The darker shades of carnelian are also more popular with gemstone bead enthusiasts. Personally, I prefer those that border on brown rather than burgundy.

✔ **Citrine:** The citrine gemstone is a birthstone for the month of November. It is a form of quartz and is normally a translucent light to dark yellow color.

✔ **Coral:** Coral is an organic gem created by animal organisms from the ocean. Its colors range from light orange to dark red. It can be very expensive. Some coral is not legally farmed, so faux coral is a good alternative. Faux coral is normally made from glass or resin.

✔ **Emerald:** This is a precious stone, so emerald beads can be very pricey. It is also a delicate stone, so it can fracture fairly easily. Another favorite of fine jewelers, you'll normally find faceted emeralds in gold jewelry. However, some vendors also sell emerald beads.

✔ **Fluorite:** When you purchase fluorite beads, you'll notice that they don't come in just one color. In fact, if you buy them by the unfinished strand, you'll see that even on one strand, the colors vary from light to dark purple, light to dark green, and off-white. Look for similar pairs of beads to make funky earrings. Or string various colors together with spacer beads to show off the variety available.

✔ **Garnets:** Garnet is the birthstone for January. While you've probably seen this used in fine jewelry before, it is also a very popular and fairly inexpensive gemstone used for beads as well. It comes in a variety of colors, but normally, you most often find garnet beads to be dark red to burgundy in color.

✔ **Hematite:** Dark and shiny, hematite is an iron ore. It is dark gray and to some people, it looks black. Along with round beads in different millimeters, hematite beads are also available in a variety of shapes such as stars, hearts, cubes, moons, and tubes. I use teardrops often for earrings or pendants.

✔ **Iolite:** Originating from the mineral cordierite, it's a violet blue gemstone often with ribbons and flecks of other colors. It's recently surged in popularity. Some of the areas where this gemstone is mined include Sri Lanka, India, and Burma. Pair it with rose quartz or freshwater pearls to create a delicate bracelet or pair of earrings.

✔ **Jade:** Reminiscent of the Orient, jade is a very hard stone and has been used for centuries for carving. Dark green is the most common form of jade, but it also comes in other colors such as lavender, yellow, and orange.

✔ **Jasper:** This highly prized gemstone of the ancient world is still popular today. It's found in many different colors, but each displays ribbons of color, which make it a favorite of *lapidary artists,* or jewelry stonecutters. Look for beautiful cabochons, pendants, and beads in various shapes made from this beautiful stone.

- **Lapis lazuli:** This is a beautiful blue stone with flecks of pyrite infused throughout. The darker the color, the higher the quality of the lapis lazuli. It looks really nice when combined with southwestern related stones such as malachite and turquoise. I personally prefer to pair lapis lazuli with sterling silver, rather than gold, findings and spacers.

- **Mother-of-pearl:** This is actually a form of shell, and while it is available in it's natural color (a mixture of beiges), most beaders like to use the white variety of mother-of-pearl beads, which have been bleached to a pearly white color. If you want the look of pearls without the price, these are a good economic alternative to consider.

- **Peridot:** The birthstone for those born in August, peridot is a form of olivine, and its richest deposits come from the island of Zagbargad. Legends claim that this pale green stone was a favorite of Cleopatra.

- **Rock crystal:** Clear quartz is commonly called rock crystal. Though it can be found in a number of different types of beads including beautiful pendants, it's also very popular as chip beads, which are (as the name implies) small chips of stone with holes in them.

- **Rose quartz:** Very often rose quartz, which is a light pink, is color treated because in its natural form it is a very pale pink color. Like most quartz stones, don't leave it in bright light or the color will fade.

- **Serpentine:** Usually in bead form, serpentine is light green, but this stone also comes in yellow, brown, and black. It is mined all over the world. A few countries that actively mine this stone include Italy, Canada, and Russia.

- **Tanzanite:** Tanzanite is named after the location where it was discovered, Tanzania in East Africa. It's a beautiful purple color with overtones of blue. Tanzanite is tough to get and extremely expensive because civil war has ravaged Tanzania for decades. If you want the look of tanzanite, look for other stones, like zoisite, that are heated to create a version of tanzanite.

- **Tiger's eye:** Tiger's eye is an earthy-colored stone with streaks of light to dark brown and golden yellows throughout. A few areas in which it is found include Australia, South Africa, and North America. This is an excellent stone to use with natural fibers such as leather and hemp.

- **Tourmaline:** This distinction doesn't refer to one type of stone but rather a group of ten different minerals. When purchasing tourmaline beads, you'll find these most often available in colors of pink, orangey red, blues, and green. Tourmaline is beautiful in pendants and earrings.

- **Turquoise:** Turquoise is used in much of the jewelry made in the southwest, which is understandable because deposits of turquoise are located across the western part of the United States. Because it is a soft, porous stone, many turquoise beads are labeled as "stabilized," meaning it has been treated with resin to help keep the stone from breaking apart when it is carved into beads and other shapes.

If some of the stones are outside your budget, consider looking for glass versions of the stones that mimic the patterns and colors. They are often priced much lower, but they still look professional and beautiful. But remember, you can't sell them as the genuine article if they're glass. Check out the next section, "Choosing stone components," for tips on how to buy them right.

The powers of semi-precious metals and stones

Jewelry supplies aren't just beautiful; they can also have deep meanings. Much like flowers in the Victorian age, gems and metals were chosen as gifts for their healing properties, to symbolize feelings, and to send a message to the receiver. Here are a few of my favorite myths surrounding some of the stones I use:

Amazonite: Associated with love, truth, and honor. It was believed to have calming, cleansing properties.

Amethyst: Makes the wearer gentle and good-natured. It's believed to help fight addiction and prevent drunkenness. Many believe it can stabilize mental disorders bringing a healing peace and love to the wearer.

Aquamarine: Provides the calming energy of the sea. Worn by sailors to harness the power of the sea and instill bravery, it's believed to have powers of healing, bringing joy and enhancing perception.

Aventurine: Believed to increase intelligence and boost creative energy. Long a good-luck stone for gamblers, it gives good luck and brings the wearers money and protects them from theft.

Black onyx: Used for lucky talismans in battle. It's a protective stone that promotes physical and mental strength and good decision-making.

Garnet: Symbol of true friendship. It's also said to stimulate creativity and passion.

Hematite: Makes the wearer full or energy, alertness, and passion.

Jade: Luck and ancient wisdom long life, fertility, wisdom, and promotes a sense of balance.

Jasper: An ancient stone associated with healing, protection, and relaxation. Some believe it can protect the wearer from snake and spider bites.

Lapis lazuli: Heightens awareness, ESP, and creativity.

Opal: Believed to enhance memory, imagination, and creativity. It was believed to banish nightmares and bring happy dreams.

Pearls: Symbolizes purity, faith, and innocence.

Rose quartz: Brought the wearers love and happiness and linked them to the gods and the afterlife.

Sapphire: Brings the power of peace and healing, especially depression and anxiety. Sapphire is believed to fulfill dreams and desires.

Silver: Purported to be the metal of the moon.

Tiger's eye: Used as a protector of the spirit, bringer of luck and fortune. It's said to soften stubbornness.

Tourmaline: Color changing chameleon gemstone is said to hold inspirations in the ever-changing color combinations. Some call it the Muse's Stone.

Turquoise: Used by hunters to ensure their success. It absorbs negativity energy and balances male and female energies.

While beauty is in the eye of the beholder, the actual identification of a gemstone is not. Scientists and jewelers send stones through rigorous tests to identify and classify them, to make sure that if looks like a citrine, walks like a citrine, it is a citrine.

Choosing stone components

A *component* is a bead, charm, or a small piece of a larger jewelry piece. Don't be confused by terms thrown around in bead and gem stores to describe stones. Gemstones can be called *natural, genuine, synthetic, simulated, treated* — or any combination of those terms.

Here's the key to understanding common gemstone terms before buying stone components and gemstones.

✔ *Natural* gemstones are just that, 100 percent natural. They may have been cut and polished, but other than that, their beauty was created without interference from humans. Natural gemstones haven't been treated, heated, dyed, or altered by people.

✔ *Genuine* gemstones start out as natural gemstones, but they may have been treated to enhance their appearance. They may have been treated with heat or radiation to change or enhance the color of the stone. Small cracks in them may have been filled with epoxy, resin, or wax. (It's the gemological equivalent of filling dings in your car's windshield.) When any of these treatments have been applied, they are no longer natural gemstones. They are still real gems, just not natural gems.

Treating gemstones isn't a fraudulent practice. It's recognized as a legitimate procedure in the industry. Treatments allow more of us to own gemstones, because it rescues stones that would otherwise not be sellable. If naturally "perfect" stones were the only ones available, most people couldn't afford them.

✔ *Simulated* gemstones are sometimes called *imitation stones*. These stones are usually made from glass that's colored to mimic the genuine article. They can be a beautiful addition to any jewelry piece at a fraction of the cost. Watch out for simulated stones mounted in a setting that may have either foil or paint behind it, to change its appearance. Ask the jeweler about the mounting, and if you have any doubts have them remove the mounting and examine the stone on its own. A cubic zirconia, or CZ, is a simulated stone.

✔ *Synthetic* gemstones are grown in a lab. In fact, they're sometimes called *lab-grown* stones. They aren't dug out of the ground. They are created by heating minerals and components to precise temperatures. Synthetic gemstones share the same physical, chemical, and optical properties. In fact, in order to use these terms, the Federal Trade Commission (FTC) requires that the stone be identical in everyway to the natural version. Many synthetic gems are tough to detect unless you're an expert.

✔ A *composite* stone is a smaller piece or slice of a desirable, genuine stone that's been combined with a larger chunk of an inexpensive or imitation gemstone. In the case of opals, sometimes thin slices of opal are placed on top of cheaper quartz pieces. These stones can be beautiful, just make sure you know what it is and are paying an appropriate price for it.

Not all genuine stones are valuable. Poor quality stones are lurking out there, so be aware. Poor quality, but genuine, stones are available at inflated prices. Get the facts about a specific gem before you buy it. Buy pricey gemstones labeled *natural* only from an experienced jeweler or store you trust. If you're buying a stone for its beauty rather than its traditional value, let your eye be your guide: If the price seems fair and you like the stone, go for it.

Like any other industry, supply and demand drives gemstone prices up and down. While every stone and bead is different, you can expect to pay from $5 to $50 for a 16-inch strand of 5–6mm polished round stone beads or chips and $3 to 10 for an imitation strand. If you are not set on a particular stone, but you want a particular color, you can still create a gemstone necklace at a reasonable price. Refer to Table 3-3 for tips on stone substitutions to get the look you love for a lot less.

Sourcing Your Beads, Pearls, and Stones

If you haven't already, soon you'll want to start acquiring your own personal stash of beads, stones, gems, and pearls. Take it from me, it's addicting. And to feed that addiction, er, I mean hobby, thousands of stores, Web sites, and catalogs market to beaders, jewelry makers, and crafters of all ages and ability. My best advice is to start out small and get a feel for what kind of beads you want to work with, what kind of projects you want to make, and what design elements work for your projects. Check out the following sections for my tips on finding and buying your beads in many different locations.

Finding beads in stores

Get started by going to your local bead store, bead show, or craft fair. Check out the beads, stones, and pearls. Take your time, touch the beads, feel their weight, and check out the variations in color and quality. Browse the bins of loose beads and pendants; run your fingers through the dangling strands. Look through the glass cabinets and view the expensive stuff. If you're like me, in no time, you'll be a bead nut. Michael's (www.michaels.com), Jo-Ann Fabric and Crafts (www.joann.com), and Hobby Lobby (www.hobbylobby.com) are national crafts store chains that devote entire sections of their stores and Web sites to beading and jewelry making. Along with all the necessary tools and storage things you need, they carry small packets of semi-precious stones and freshwater pearls, plus plenty of simulated glass and plastic beads for fun. They are a great resource if you just want a small quantity to try things out.

When selecting individual beads, look for focal point pieces for your creations and choose items that appeal to me. You may see an individual bead in the store and have it inspire your design. So, walk around bead stores. Check out the carved quartz or jade pendants, Italian glass rosettes, faceted briolets, crystal, or gemstone drops. Refer to Figure 3-4 for a representation of made different shapes and cuts of stones. And be sure to check out the "Identifying man-made beads" section earlier in this chapter for information on the different kinds of beads available and my recommendations for how to use them.

Buying in bulk via the Internet

When you're ready to do some serious buying and feel confident about what you want, it's always cheaper (and more convenient) to buy in bulk. If you're buying from a catalog, many have a $25 to $50 minimum order, plus shipping, so buying in bulk definitely pays off. You get more beads at a lower price per bead, plus you often save on the shipping costs.

Consider buying the following items in bulk:

- ✔ Clear AB crystals of any size (but get as many 4mm and 6mm as you can afford, because the smaller quantities of these sizes get expensive very quickly)

- ✔ Pearls, both cultured and faux

- ✔ Findings, including earwires, headpins, crimp beads, and any other basics (see Chapter 2)

- ✔ Miscellaneous beads, plus glass beads, seed beads, and metal spacer beads, in neutral colors and shapes

- ✔ Stringing materials, including metal wire and nylon thread

Consider your own projects and designs when you make your own list of items to buy in bulk. If you are interested in honing your skills in Native American jewelry, purchasing some turquoise beads in bulk, for example, may be a perfect solution for you.

Avoiding common mistakes: Take it easy!

Just because it's cheaper to buy in bulk doesn't mean you have to buy more than you need, so measure out what your needs are first! If you're starting a jewelry-making business, find a balance with your *cash flow,* or the amount of money coming in versus the amount of money going out. Because jewelry making and beading is so fun, it's easy to forget that you need to sell your creations to get money to buy more supplies. For more information on starting a jewelry business, take a gander at Chapter 14.

If you order something and change your mind, save it for later. You may need it. If you really hate it, though, by all means send it back fast, before you forget where you put it.

Buyer beware. Many of these items, especially beads, may not be returnable, so choose a reputable vendor and ask about its return and refund policy before giving your credit card number. Ask whether the vendor refunds shipping costs as well. Many don't, even if they do accept returned merchandise.

Keep all your beads in the original packaging until you're sure you are keeping them. It's tough to sort through subtle size and color differences between beads after they get mixed up. And most bead vendors won't take returns if you've opened the bulk packaging.

As always on the Internet, make sure the Web site you visit offers a secure order form before you give any personal information. If it makes you feel better, get the customer service number and call it. I have used many of the vendors listed in this book, and they offer unconditional service.

If you have a bead budget, stick to it. Promise you'll only spend $50 and no more because, like anything else, jewelry making can be addictive. Take it from a bead nut!

Getting the most for your money

Buying in bulk always gets you the best price, but again, don't buy excessively more than you need. I don't want to hear about your 10 metric tons of crystals sitting in your attic for the next half-century if you're not going to at least enjoy it! Worse case, your grandkids can always sell your beads on eBay.

If you're in a small bead boutique or at bead show, know what you're buying and realize that your beads are likely not refundable. So enjoy!

Always read the fine print in the catalog or on the Web site. If you're in doubt, call and ask customer service for details that could impact your buying. Many beads and stones look alike and have similar names, and that can be confusing.

For example, hemalyke is the simulated (manmade) version of the natural semi-precious stone hematite. If you want (and pay for) the genuine article, make sure you get it.

Going to bead and gem shows

After your hobby kicks into high gear, visit a local bead show. Check out the local paper if you're traveling for business or pleasure. You may find several shows taking place at any given time of the year. And definitely don't forget to look in jewelry and bead related magazines. Most big shows post ads in them months ahead of time.

Going to shows is a great time to look for unusual or centerpiece beads. You get a chance to look at a wide variety of beads to find the perfect ones for future projects. Take a look at Project 3-2, Floating Stone Drop Necklace, for an easy way to use a perfect stone.

Finding shows

Finding shows may be easier than you think. Here are our ideas for finding them:

- ✓ Check out the events listings in your local paper; it may mention bead and gem shows. Sometimes the bead show is combined with an antiques mart, crafts fair, or even an art festival.

- ✓ Look for updates and notices about shows in crafts and bead stores. Ask the staff for details.

- ✓ Do a search on the Internet for "bead and gem shows" and see what's in your area.

- ✓ Browse the *Lapidary Journal* magazine, which features a monthly bead/gem show calendar, or visit www.lapidaryjournal.com.

- ✓ The Tucson International Bead and Gem Show is the largest of its kind in the world. Check its Web site for show dates and events: www.tucson showguide.com/tsg.

- ✓ Check out your local beads society. For a complete state-by-state listing of registered bead societies, go to www.lapidaryjournal.com, and then pull down the site directory box and go to bead societies.

Making the most of your time at the show

At the show, check the show schedule guide and exhibit map before cruising the show floor to avoid wasting time. It's beautiful to see so many gems in one place and fun to talk to all the distributors, but these shows can be are massive and very tiring, so conserve your energy and have fun.

Sometimes ads and Web sites for the shows offer coupons to print from your computer or cut out from the paper. You may score a free bag of crystals or a storage jar for your beads.

Go to the show early to see the fullest inventory. You'll likely enjoy them with the biggest crowds of the show. Better yet, make a vacation out of the show. Do some sightseeing afterwards if you're visiting Tucson, for example.

Project 3-2: Floating Stone Drop Necklace

For something dramatic but understated, a floating stone drop necklace is an easy project to create, fun to wear, and one you'll have for a long time.

Depending on your budget and level of confidence, choose any size stone as your centerpiece, from a 2-inch smooth aventurine or faceted rose quartz briolet, with a vertical drilled hole. Choose a stone with a large enough hole to accommodate a double thickness of your stringing material. Check out Figure 3-11 to see the finished project.

Tools and Materials

1 flat-nose pliers

Scissors

Satin cord, silk ribbon, or thin leather cord, cut to desired necklace length

1 large center stone drilled vertically (use bead reamer if thread or cord doesn't fit through hole)

1 large (but smaller than the center stone) accent stone, drilled vertically

1. **Thread one side of cord through smaller accent bead.** I used a silver bead and leather cord in my project. Situate the bead so that so that cord is evenly divided on both sides of the bead. See Figure 3-10a.

2. **Thread two sides of cord through large center bead so that the small bead sits directly underneath the larger center bead, and that both sides of the cord are equal length.** See Figure 3-10b.

3. **Secure the cord around the toggle clasp by tying and knotting it. Trim away any excess cord.**

4. **Close the clasps, put around your neck, and feel the calming energy take effect.**

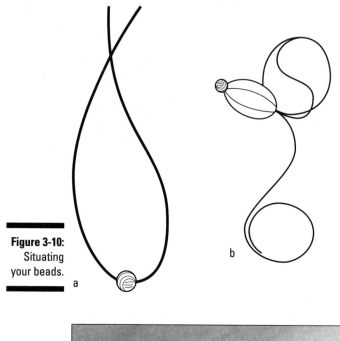

Figure 3-10:
Situating
your beads.

a

b

Figure 3-11:
Floating
Stone Drop
Necklace.

Chapter 4

Creating Your Jewelbox: Setting Up Your Workshop

. . . .

In This Chapter

▶ Choosing the right spot for your workshop

▶ Laying out your equipment

▶ Organizing your supplies

▶ Setting up a safe space

▶ Making sure your home is ready

. . . .

*W*hether you design jewelry as a business or are just simply dabbling here and there, you need to set up a workspace that fosters creativity, serenity, productivity, and most importantly, ensures your personal (and family's) safety. The more you can plan and think about your space before-hand, the easier, more pleasant, and cost-effective your jewelry-making experi-ence will be.

In this chapter, I outline several options for making the most of the space (and time) you have. I show you how to select the best spot in your home for your workshop and get your equipment and supplies organized right. I also show you how to plan your shop with safety in mind. And finally, I help you kid-proof your space, in case you happen to have a nosy toddler around.

Setting Up Your Workshop

In most cases, you don't have the luxury of having a separate artist's studio to lock yourself away for uninterrupted hours. So try to find a quiet space as far away from the rest of your house (and anyone else who lives there) as possi-ble. Avoid distractions like the phone, refrigerator, and TV. It doesn't really matter how big the space is, but choose a place where you can get away from the daily grind. A cozy corner, an empty guest room, or a well-ventilated and finished basement, attic, or garage are all potential workshop sites. Here are a few more practical tips to help you choose the right spot for you:

- ✔ **Decide whether you want to choose a spot with a view or near a window.** What inspires some distracts others. If you choose a spot near a window, add blinds or a shade, just in case you do want to close yourself off, although many jewelry makers think natural lighting is best.

  You'll probably also need additional lighting depending on the time of day you work, the weather, and so on. If natural light isn't possible, consider choosing natural light bulbs. Take a look at "Taking lighting into account," later in this chapter for information on which bulbs to get.

- ✔ **Make sure you have adequate heat, ventilation, and air-conditioning for your climate.** I'm always more creative when I'm truly comfortable.

  Ventilation is particularly important in jewelry making to prevent breathing the tiny particles of dust and glass that can accumulate during some jewelry-making processes, like stone cutting, lampwork, and designing with polymer clay. If you're working strictly with stringing beads and wire wrapping, ventilation isn't as critical.

- ✔ **If you can't find a dedicated spot for your workshop (or if your space is pretty small), create a moveable workshop.** Buy a rolling cart with drawers at any housewares store, like Bed, Bath & Beyond (www.bedbathand beyond.com) or Linens 'N' Things (www.lnt.com), so that you can simply roll your supplies over to the dining room table and tuck them away when you're finished. Check out Figure 4-1 for a peek at what this looks like.

- ✔ **Choose a quiet spot.** If that's not possible, get a radio and play soft music or jazz to drown out the noise. Unplug the phones if you can, even for an hour. If you really want or need to dampen the noise, you can purchase acoustic foam sheets that screw into your walls to soundproof your space and protect your office from distraction. Check out your local music store or Web site geared to studio musicians for information on where to get acoustic foam in your area.

  Turn off the TV. If you do get inspiration from designs worn by your favorite soap opera stars or TV entertainment magazines, of course, watch them. Just don't do it in your workshop. Watch them at different times with a sketchbook or notebook in hand to jot down design ideas. When you're actually designing, the TV is just a brain sucker.

- ✔ **For security, safety, and, well, privacy, try to have a lock on the door.** This step keeps nosy toddlers, pets, and other curious life forms out of the area while you're not in your workshop.

  If you do purchase expensive gemstones and precious metal, keep them locked in a safe and keep your office locked for double protection.

✔ **Choose the color for your paint and accessories wisely.** Create your own peaceful retreat, with light browns, sage greens, or calming blues. Add punches of color for interest, but keep the overall feeling relaxed. My office/workshop has textured walls that I study when I need a brain break or need to rest my eyes from designing.

Figure 4-1:
Rolling cart.

Assessing your cubic working space

Size doesn't matter — when you're talking about your workspace, I mean. It's the quality of the space that counts and how you use it. If you've found several good potential work spots in your house, the hardest part will be choosing one!

But, first a few things to get your started right before you move in to your new space:

✔ **Clear away all clutter.** Toss empty boxes, old newspapers, and odds and ends. Get rid of it now. Sell it, recycle it, dump it, whatever you need to do, but don't keep it around. It's tough to get inspired with a pile of stuff you've been trying to find time to go through for the last ten years staring you in the face. Check out *Organizing For Dummies* by Eileen Roth and Elizabeth Miles (Wiley) for great tips on pairing down your junk — er, I mean, your stuff — and organizing the rest of it.

✔ **Measure your freshly cleared space with a measuring tape.** Write down the dimensions so you'll have them in case you need to order a desk, chairs, shelves, storage containers, and so on. Make sure to measure the height of the ceilings and your windows (including the distance from top of the window to the floor and the bottom of the window to the floor). You may want to add window treatments or blinds to your relaxing new space.

Buy a soft retractable measuring tape if you don't already have one. You can find this product in the sewing department of your local crafts or fabric store. They're handy to have around for measuring your jewelry and components and the necks, wrists, and other body parts of your clients. One costs about $2.

Taking lighting into account

Eyestrain can become a problem as you spend time looking at delicate pieces of jewelry. To minimize the problem, rely primarily on natural light, if at all possible, but other sources can be used if natural light isn't available or adequate for you.

Full-spectrum light bulbs mimic natural light. They provide a whiter, brighter light, but use less energy than other bulbs. They also reduce eyestrain and glare, and can improve your overall sense of well-being. Full spectrum light helps you see the true colors of beads, gems, and stones you're working with. GE Reveal bulbs are full-spectrum light bulbs available in just about any hardware, discount, or housewares store, but many other brands are available, including Chromalux and Bulbrite.

Choosing a lamp

Halogen lamps emit bright white light and are available in many styles. But they can get a hot if left on too long, and they pose a fire hazard if knocked over. Check out the halogen lamps in your local housewares store, but if you buy one, use them with care. Keep them set as low as possible and always turn them off if they're unattended.

If you like the lamps you already have, try replacing their bulbs with full-spectrum incandescent or fluorescent bulbs, like GE Reveal bulbs. You can also buy a lamp with a magnifier or an eyepiece with a magnifier and light, if you prefer. I use an adjustable lamp that can be moved around at a whim. I have to say, though, that I move it much less now that I use full-spectrum bulbs.

If you do opt to buy a lamp specifically for jewelry making and beading, do some online research first because so many styles are available. You can find anything from portable, folding lamps to full lighting systems designed with crafters and artists in mind. Your options are almost limitless.

Consider buying a lamp with a magnifying glass attached to it. Swing it in when you need it, or move it out of the way when you don't. It may be more comfortable than wearing a heavy eyepiece.

Room lighting

Whenever possible, natural sunlight is best. But if you're like me and have to do much of your work at night, natural sunlight isn't an option. Choose a room that has recessed overhead halogen or incandescent lights, if possible. If not, get a large floor lamp and two table lamps.

I prefer to set the room lights up on a dimmer that allows me to adjust the overhead lights to my preferred level. I set the one in my workshop up with a remote control, so I can make adjustments from my desk (where I'm actually working) to see how the light change affects the project. It sounds fancy, but it cost me only $40 at my local hardware store.

Undertaking your quest for the perfect chair

Like your eyes, your back and neck need protection from the strain that the close work of jewelry design requires. Chairs can be pretty pricey, and there are hundreds of models out there from backless ergonomic chairs to bouncy chairs to cushy chairs that move all over the place . . . the choices are mind-boggling. That said, visit your local office-supply store to try the chairs and see what feels most comfortable first. Write down the information about the chairs you like and their prices, and then hit the streets to do your comparison shopping.

Check the back of your favorite beading magazine, even jewelry supply catalogs, for ads for comfortable crafting chairs. Or try Web sites like `http://healthyback.com` and look at ergonomically friendly kneeling-style chair designs, like the one in Figure 4-2. Depending on what the chair is made from, one like this can cost between $100 and $200, but it's worth every penny. Plus it sports a very compact design, which is ideal if you have limited space.

If you're not into it's ultra-modern design, try an ergonomic chair with a back-rest and wheels, instead. Be sure to place a plastic pad underneath if you have plush carpeting. It makes it much easier to move around your workspace.

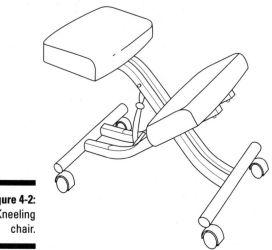

Figure 4-2:
Kneeling
chair.

Choosing a desk or table

If you're actually buying a desk specifically for jewelry making, consider an L-shaped desk, which is available at very low cost and in dozens of styles and colors at Staples, Office Depot, Office Max, or just about any office-supply store. You can put your office files in the drawer (if you have any), a small computer in the corner (if you need to share space with one), your beading supplies on the long side, and you're all set.

While a drafting table with a slightly slanted top may seem like another good option, the beads will end up on your lap, so a flat desktop is your best option.

If your feet get crampy when you're sitting for a long period of time, buy an angled footrest. They are inexpensive (about $15–$30), and they work like a charm!

When sitting at your desk, be sure your knees are at a 60-degree to 90-degree angle, with your hands gently resting in front of you, at, or slightly above your waist. Play with the chair height to see what works. You may have to prop your desk up a bit. This posture helps prevent *carpal tunnel syndrome,* a painful wrist and hand condition that can occur in people who work in awkward positions and overuse their hands. Check out Figure 4-3 for good posture for sitting and working long hours.

Figure 4-3:
Good
posture
helps you
stay
comfortable
while you
work.

Making sure you're covered: Thinking about flooring

Whether your place has hardwood floors, rugs, carpeting, or a combination of all of these, it's important to consider flooring when choosing where to design your jewelry, because you'll be spending a lot of time chasing tiny beads. Most beading nuts (like me) prefer carpeting or rugs, because they keep the beads you'll inevitably drop from rolling away. If using carpeting or a rug isn't possible, throw a large towel underneath your chair for faster cleanup at the end of the day.

Cover the end of your vacuum cleaner tube with a pair of old pantyhose. The vacuum's suction will pull the beads off the floor, and the pantyhose will trap them so they can't go into the vacuum.

Setting Up Your Tools

See Chapter 2 for more information about supplies and tools; this section helps you organize them.

Efficiency is the name of the game

All the creativity in the world doesn't mean a thing if you're not efficient and able to carry out your ideas and dreams. With that in mind, you may have to experiment to see what works best for you. If you don't need an official work pad and prefer to work directly on a hard surface, go for it. Maybe you prefer to just put a towel down. But be sure you have all the tools, supplies, and beads you need close by and handy so you don't have to keep getting up. Try to have everything in front of you within easy sight and access.

Cleanliness equals perfection

Keeping your workspace clean and tidy not only increases your efficiency, but it also prevents accidents. Set aside some time, either at the end of the day or the beginning of the next, to tidy and clean up. I recommend cleaning at the end of your day, so that you can start fresh the next.

There isn't one "right" way to clean your studio, but you need to do it often. On your desk, use a portable vacuum, or wipe clean with a damp cloth or an electrostatic dust cloth, like a Swiffer or Pledge Grab-It. Either will pick up, not just redistribute, dust and small debris.

 Electrostatic dust cloths, like the Swiffer or Pledge Grab-It, are a fantastic innovation for home cleaning developed in the last few years. Dust, dirt, and debris cling to the cloths, rather than just falling to the floor or getting redistributed into the air, making the cloths easy to throw away later.

Odds and ends

Just in case you need to sort something new, keep an extra stash of bags or even little kid-sized paper cups on hand. They're great for easy access, and are useful for when you involve your children in the jewelry-making process. Check out Chapter 13 for the full story on making jewelry with kids.

Containing Gems and More

If you are not the most organized person on earth, this is the section for you. Sort your gems as soon as you buy them, because you may never get around to it later. For easy and cheap sorting and storage, you can't beat resealable plastic bags. Get them in every size now, especially the mini or snack size. You can find specific jewelry-sized bags (roughly 2×3 inches) online or at the craft or jewelry store. Use these if you have just a few of a special kind of bead. Use them as easy way to store small finished projects.

Separate all your beads, pearls, stones, and gems, by size, color, shape, style — whatever makes them different from each other. If you have so many that organizing trays are unmanageable, put each kind of bead in a resealable plastic bag. Then get a large plastic tub with a snap-on lid. Place all the bags in the tub.

For even more security, keep the tub in a locking file drawer. Again, to keep out those nosy housemates and family members, if you have any.

Bead nuts usually love the cute little storage boxes and neat sorting trays available at crafts stores, and I find that this is one of the best parts of designing jewelry. For some fun recommendations check out the next few sections.

Bead board organizer

Used for stringing necklaces, a gray bead board organizer has space for three strands, and is calibrated in inches for easy designing and measuring. A white version is made for single strand projects and costs about $6.75 each online. You may be able to find them cheaper at your local bead store. I picked one up just the other day for under $3. If you think you may travel with your supplies, consider purchasing a bead board case and portable bead organizer called the Bead Buddy, available for about $30. It's a great and very useful gadget. Check out Figure 4-4 for a peek at several bead board organizers.

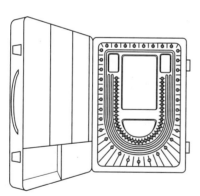

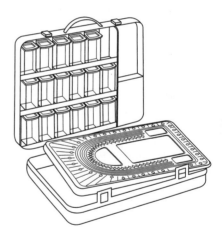

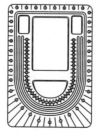

Figure 4-4:
Bead board
organizers.

Sorting trays

If you stop into any office-supply, hardware, fishing tackle, crafts, or beading supply store, you'll find a vast array of plastic sorting trays, some with lids, some with screw caps, some that fold. Choose whatever style, size, and shape suits you, but I prefer the plain and simple clear organizer box with 15 to 18 little compartments and a few larger dividers to hold tools. They cost about $4–$7 each. Buy several; you'll use 'em. Next, check out the vials or little stacking space saver jars, like the ones shown in Figure 4-5. They come six jars per set and cost $3 each; a package of ten vials will set you back about $4.

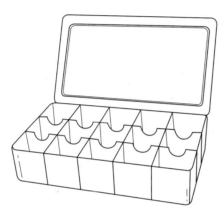

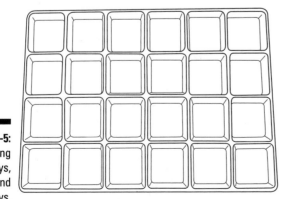

Figure 4-5:
Organizing
boxes, trays,
jars, and
funnel trays.

Invest in some small triangular metal trays. They nest together and have sloped, angled edges that acts as funnels for easy cleanup. Check out Figure 4-5b to see what these nifty gadgets look like.

When you're finished at night but still in the middle of a project, be sure to gently cover your work with a heavy cloth or towel, in case a curious pet, gust of wind, or some other disaster sweeps away your one-of-a-kind creation. That said, remember to keep the windows in your workshop closed, the alarm on, and/or the door locked.

Practicing Safety First

Safety in the workshop is a serious effort. It requires taking large measures as well as always paying attention to the little details. Whenever people get into any routine, it's easy to be complacent and forget about standard safety precautions. Jewelry making is no exception. The way to avoid this is to simply pay attention to what you are doing.

Protecting your eyes should always be your top priority, not only from invasive flying debris, but from strain as well. Besides proper lighting, a magnifier headpiece, such as an Optivisor, acts both as a basic shield and as protection from strain. But for procedures such as polishing or making bead holes, you should wear safety goggles or glasses. Purchase an Optivisor through any bead maker's catalog or from the back of jewelry-making magazines like *Lapidary Journal.*

After you start doing detail work, you may notice more eyestrain. One of the most important and most basic things you can do to protect your eyesight is to see your ophthalmologist at least once a year. Also consider using an eyepiece.

Keeping the volume of background noise low will be healthier for your ears and still allow you to hear any unusual sounds.

Here are a few general safety tips to keep in mind in your workshop:

- **Keep your hands clean.** Make sure any wound is clean and protected from further damage. Keep a box of baby wipes handy and accessible in your workshop. Make sure your tetanus shots are up to date.

- **Keep a good first aid kit nearby.** Ready-made kits are available from most drugstores or you can build your own.

  Must-haves for your first aid kit include the following:

  - Sterile adhesive bandages

  - Antibacterial ointment

  - Antiseptic (like hydrogen peroxide) or antibacterial moist towelettes

- Sterile gauze pads

- Adhesive strips

- Knuckle bandages

- Cooling burn gel

- Acetaminophen or ibuprofen

- Scissors

✔ **Keep a trash can nearby** to dispose of any loose ends, wire pieces, and broken beads, with one hand.

✔ **Restrict access to your workspace,** keeping out kids, pets, and anybody else.

✔ **Be sure the electrical system in your studio is safe.** Don't overload any one circuit, and use extension cords only when absolutely necessary. Purchase a power strip with surge protection built in. It will cut the power if the circuit does become overloaded, saving your equipment, your wiring, and your body from an unfortunate accident.

✔ **Be careful with drinks on your desk.** Spills are one issue, but you don't want to get bits of wire, pieces of glass, and so on into your beverage. It's definitely not a good idea to ingest debris from your supplies.

✔ **After you put on your safety glasses and mask, get anything loose or dangling out of the way.** Tie back loose hair, secure clothing, and remove dangling jewelry.

When using glue, check the labels to be sure of the safety precautions. Some glues are poisonous, and some glues have fumes that are hazardous to children and pregnant women. Remember to store glue containers out of sight of children and pets, as in a dark and cool place.

Is Your Home Ready? A Checklist

Here is a planning checklist that identifies important considerations, must-have equipment, and basic supplies you need:

✔ **Have you identified a distinct location for your workshop?** You'll be more productive if you have a clear boundary that isolates your work space from the phone, noise, and interruptions. The boundary can be a door, a couch, or a curtain.

✔ **Is there adequate electrical support to support your anticipated designs?** Do you have enough outlets for your drill press, your sander, and your lamp? Can you accommodate hot glue guns and a lighted magnifying glass? How about the right number of lamps?

✔ **Is there sufficient lighting in your space?** If there's not enough light, do you have the means to add enough?

✔ **Have you designed the right layout for your space?** Create a layout where you don't sit too close to a doorway, in order to avoid distraction.

✔ **Are you using your space efficiently?** Think about space saving technology and other gadgets, like stackable sorting jars. Add cheap shelving or cardboard file boxes to a closet.

✔ **Have you kid-proofed your workshop as much as possible?**

- Jewelry making often involves dangerous processes, sharp tools, and small items that are easy to swallow. Keep that in mind when cleaning up as well as setting up your space.

- Use normal parental common sense. A locked cabinet for the more dangerous items is a good idea. If you can't hire a babysitter, keep a baby gate up as a barrier, if needed.

- If you do permit your children into your studio, keep dangerous items out of reach as much as possible.

- With older kids, be straight with them about the dangers involved. Starting between 3 and 4 years old, kids can then make jewelry themselves (with your supervision, of course!). Take a look at Chapter 13 for scoop on making jewelry with children.

Part II
Discovering Simple Jewelry-Making Techniques

The 5th Wave   By Rich Tennant

"Warren! I told you to keep the WigJig under lock and key! Kevin got hold of it and he and his friend are trying to make a chain-link fence with it!"

In this part . . .

$\boldsymbol{1}$ introduce you to many basic jewelry techniques, like stringing and knotting, weaving and looming, and working with wire. I give you several projects for each technique to get you practicing today. You can create any of these projects in as little 30 minutes. So sit down, grab some tools, and start stringing!

Chapter 5

Uncovering the Simple Secrets of Stringing and Knotting

Stringing was the first jewelry technique practiced by our ancestors some 15,000 years ago. These distant relatives strung cowrie shells onto some kind of thread-like material and wore them as ornamentation and to indicate status in their community. The art of stringing is still alive and well. And in the last few thousand years or so, we've made some innovations to make the job more intricate and beautiful.

In this chapter, I show you the basics of stringing and knotting. I introduce you to the tools and materials you need to get started. I give you trendy fun projects to practice your newfound skills. And finally, I give you the lowdown to help you decide which glue is for you.

Stringing: The Basics

The term *stringing* is just what the name implies: threading beads, a pendant, or another component onto a thread of some sort. Your first piece may be something very simple like the Celtic Knot Pendant on Leather Cord in Project 1-1 in Chapter 1. Or it could be a bit more complicated like the Hematite Stretch Bracelet in Project 5-1. All you need to get started is something to string (usually beads of some sort — see Chapter 3) and something to string it on (usually cord, wire, or thread — see Chapter 2).

Project 5-1: Hematite Stretch Bracelet

This project is a great one to start with because it's stringing in its purest form. There's no clasp to work with, just a simple repetitive bead pattern that gives a simple and classic appearance. Take a look at it in Figure 5-1.

This bracelet was designed by my 12-year-old cousin, Anthony. I spent a weekend with him early in this project and turned him into a bead freak. He especially likes the magnetic hematite beads, so look for them if you can find them. For more information on making jewelry with kids, check out Chapter 13.

The knotting and gluing technique used in stretch bracelets provides for a completely seamless look. Although you won't string 12 inches of beads, I recommend you use that much because it makes knotting your bracelet much, much easier. Try it this way, and if you don't have problems tying knots with shorter ends, you can shorten the cord for you next project.

Tools and Materials

Scissors

Binder clip (the ones from the office supply store)

12 inches of 0.05 elastic beading cord, clear

10 8mm hematite hexagonal tube beads

10 5mm hematite round beads

20 3mm round beads, gold

Hypo-cement or glue of your choice

1. **Clip your binder clip to one end of your elastic.**

2. **String your beads in the following order: tube, gold, round, gold.** Continue this pattern until you've used all your beads.

3. **Remove your binder clip.** Holding both strands together, tie an overhand knot. Tie a second knot onto of the first. Dab glue on your knot. Trim away the excess elastic.

   Don't trim too close to the knot, or it will unravel.

4. **Tuck your newly glued knot inside your first tube bead.** I recommend using the tube bead to hide the knot because it's bigger than the round gold bead. Allow the glue to dry for 24 hours before wearing it.

You want a snug fit, but don't want the elastic to show. This bracelet measures approximately 7½ inches long. If this length isn't snug enough for you, feel free to make this bracelet shorter. Each set of beads (one tube bead, one round, and two gold rounds) is about ¾ inch. Remove a set of beads to make it shorter. Alternately, using smaller beads (7mm tubes and 4mm hematite rounds) would still keep the same design elements, but would shorten the bracelet about ¾ inch.

Figure 5-1:
Hematite
Stretch
Bracelet.

Knotting: Getting Started

Many fine gemstone necklaces, like those made with pearls, are individually knotted, meaning that as each gem is strung, a small knot is tied, separating it from the next one. The knots serve two purposes:

- ✔ To separate and protect the beads from rubbing against each other.
- ✔ To secure individual beads in the event the strand should break. Losing a few pearls is better than losing the whole strand.

The most important thing about knotting is getting the knots as close to the beads as possible. The beads shouldn't move around much at all between the knots. Check out the "Understanding knotting techniques" section later in this chapter for tips on how to get this done.

Using knotting materials

When bead strands are knotted, they're most likely strung on silk, satin, or nylon bead cord. Each cord comes in a variety of lengths from 2-yard cards with an attached needle to 100-foot spools without a needle. Most often, jewelry designers choose cord colors that complement the beads' colors. But, with the vast array of colors available today, many choose to use the cord as an accent.

Identifying knotting tools

To create small, tight knots close to a bead, jewelry designers use a variety of tools. You can find most of them at any beading supply store or Web site. If your local store doesn't have one of these tools, ask if they can order it for you.

Here are a few of the most common knot helpers:

- ✔ **Knotting tweezers:** These tweezers function and look much like the same tweezers you use to remove splinters or pluck errant eyebrows. But they have very small, pointed ends, terrific for holding and moving small knots. Take a look at them in Figure 5-2a.

- ✔ **Beading awl:** A beading awl looks sort of like a tiny ice pick. It often has a wooden handle, and a long, thin, sharp tip, designed to help you get into small, tight places, like inside a bead or a tiny knot. Check it out in Figure 5-2b.

- ✔ **Tri-cord knotter:** The most expensive option is the tool designed specifically for the task. I don't knot enough jewelry to make it worth the expense, which is anywhere from $50 to $120 for a kit and instructional video. But it may save you some time if you plan to do a lot of knotting. Take an up-close look in Figure 5-2c.

- ✔ **Corsage pin:** For the occasional or beginning knotter, using a corsage pin gets the job done. These pins, shown in Figure 5-2d, are stronger than standard sewing pins and won't bend under the pressure of pushing a knot along a strand.

Understanding knotting techniques

The key to good knotting is getting the knot as close as possible to the bead, so that the knots keep the beads in place, without movement. This section gives you a few different techniques for getting that done.

In each technique section, I assume that you've already started your strand, so I'm not going to spend time telling your how to tie on bead tips, clasps, or other findings. I focus only on the actual knotting technique. If you need help getting your strand started, check out Steps 2 through 4 in Project 5-2 later in this chapter.

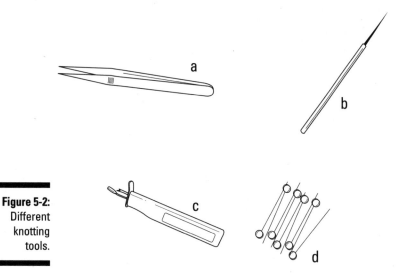

Figure 5-2:
Different
knotting
tools.

Traditional knotting

Traditional knotting is a time-consuming process, but it's definitely worth the effort. It adds an elegant element to your finished piece, particularly when you're using fine stones and gems.

Here's how to do it:

1. **After your strand is started, tie a loose knot in your cord, like the one in Figure 5-3a.**

2. **Insert the end of your pin, awl, or tweezers into the knot, as shown in Figure 5-3b.** (I use a corsage pin when I knot, so that's what you see in the illustration.)

3. **With the pin inserted, move the knot down toward the bead. Get it as close to the bead as possible. Tighten the knot down, but not all the way down, with the pin still inserted.** Take a look at Figure 5-3c to see how this looks.

4. **Remove the pin from the knot. Use the pin to move the almost-tight knot into its final place. Tighten it completely.**

Double-strand knotting

Some purists think this style of knotting is cheating or faking. I prefer to think of it as clever. It works well for fully beaded strands, but it doesn't work for Tin Cup–style necklaces, like the one in Project 5-2. If the cord isn't covered in beads, you see both strands, which isn't the look you're going for.

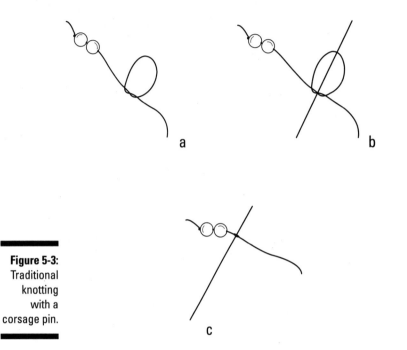

Figure 5-3:
Traditional
knotting
with a
corsage pin.

Here's how to take the easy way out:

1. **Start your strand with 2 cords, each with a needle attached. Thread both needles through one bead. Tie an overhand knot as shown in Figure 5-4a.**

2. **Tighten the knot down snugly against your bead.** Take a look at Figure 5-4b. Repeat as needed.

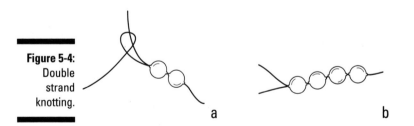

Figure 5-4:
Double
strand
knotting.

Project 5-2: Tin Cup Necklace

Movies have been spawning fashion trends since the beginning of, well, movies. *Tin Cup,* the 1996 movie starring Renee Russo and Kevin Costner, started a jewelry trend that's become a classic, hence the Tin Cup necklace. To be a Tin Cup necklace, a necklace must be made of *bead stations,* sections that contain beads, and cord sections, the gaps between the bead stations.

The cord sections can be made of just about anything (like chain, leather, or ribbon). The original necklaces were made with silk bead cord, which is what I used in this project.

I used blue sodalite beads for my necklace. Sodalite has the color of a milky navy blue with gray swirls. I chose gray cord to complement it. My necklace is approximately 17 inches long. Take a look at Figure 5-5 to see the finished product.

Tools and Materials

Corsage pin, beading awl, or knotting tweezers

Scissors

Flat-nose pliers

Round-nose pliers

Ruler

Iron (optional)

1 card of gray silk bead cord, size no. 4, needle attached

Hypo-cement, or the glue of your choice

5 8mm sodalite round beads

10 4mm bicone crystals, AB

2 clamshell bead tips, silver

2 jump rings, silver

1 lobster claw clasp, small

1. **Remove all the cord from the bead card.** It may seem like a lot of cord to work with, but if you start your strand to the bottom, you can keep the needle attached to the left over cord. Waste not, want not. I can get at least three necklaces from a single card this way.

2. **Because your cord will be kinked from being wrapped around the card, lightly iron it to straighten it out.** Use the silk setting with a dry iron.

   If you're completely opposed to ironing, you can drape your finished project around a doorknob for a few days and let gravity and the weight of the beads help you straighten it out. I'm impatient, so I iron it.

3. **Tie a knot at the end of your bead cord. Add a dab of glue to the knot. Trim away any excess cord with your scissors.**

   Don't tie your knot on the same end where you needle is. Tie it at the opposite end.

4. **String a bead tip onto your cord.** Because you want your bead tip to cover the knot you're going to tie, make sure you insert the needle through the clamshell's mouth. Slide it to the bottom to cover the knot. Using your flat-nose pliers, close the bead tip around the knot. Take a look at Chapter 8 if you need help with this step.

5. **Measure down 4 inches from on your bead tip. Tie an overhand knot.**

6. **Slide one crystal, one round bead, and one crystal. Tie a loose overhand knot (after the last crystal). Using your corsage pin, gently slide the loose knot toward the beads, making sure the beads are stacked**

tightly together. Slide the knot right next to your last bead, snugly. Remove your pin from the knot, and then use the pin to slide the knot as close to the last bead as you can. You've completed your first bead station. If you need help with the knotting techniques, refer to Figure 5-3.

7. **Measure 1 inch down from the last knot of you beads station. Tie an overhand knot.** Repeat Step 5 four times, to create a total of five bead stations.

8. **String a bead tip onto your cord.** Make sure that the mouth of the bead tip is facing away from your beads.

9. **Measure 4 inches from your last knot. Tie an overhand knot. (Note that your bead tip should be between the bead stations and the final knot.) Add a dab of glue to the knot. Using your flat-nose pliers, close the bead tip around the knot.** Chapter 8 shows you pictures to follow if you need help with bead tips.

10. **Attach the loop of one bead tip to one jump ring. Using your round-nose pliers, close the loop around the jump ring.**

11. **Using your pliers, open the other jump ring. Slide the loop of the lobster claw onto the jump ring. Close the jump ring.** See Chapter 7 for techniques on opening and closing jump rings.

12. **Connect the loop of the last bead tip to the jump ring you connected to the lobster claw in Step 11.**

Figure 5-5:
Traditional knotting techniques help you create this easy, trendy Tin Cup Necklace.

Project 5-3: Elegant Crystal and Freshwater Pearl Bracelet

This bracelet works up very quickly when you use the double strand knotting technique. I chose darker color crystals and black bead cord. The larger knots created with this technique almost look like spacer beads, adding to the design. Take a look at the finished piece in Figure 5-7.

Tools and Materials

Scissors

Flat-nose pliers

Round-nose pliers

2 cards of black silk bead cord, size no. 2, needles attached

Hypo-cement, or the glue of your choice

11 6mm fresh water pearls, oval

2 6mm bicone crystals, jet

2 6mm bicone crystals, black diamond

4 6mm bicone crystals, light Colorado topaz

4 6mm bicone crystals, smoky topaz

2 clamshell bead tips, gold-filled

1 toggle clasp, gold-filled

1. **Remove all the cord from both bead cards.**

2. **Holding both cords, tie an overhand knot at the end of your bead cords. (The knot should be at the end opposite from the end with the attached needles.) Add a dab of glue to the knot. Trim away any excess cord with your scissors.**

3. **Using both needles, string a bead tip onto your cord, with the clamshell mouth facing the knot, away from where the beads will be. Slide it to the bottom to cover the knot. Using your flat-nose pliers, close the bead tip around the knot.** Take a look at Chapter 8 if you need help with this step.

4. **Using both cords, tie an overhand knot next to the bead tip. String one smoky topaz crystal on both cords. Slide the crystal tight up against the knot.**

5. **Tie another overhand knot, snugly next to the crystal.** If you need help with this step, refer to Figure 5-4.

6. **String on a fresh water pearl on both your strands. Slide it down snugly next to the knot.** Repeat Step 5.

7. **Continue alternating between crystals and pearls, tying knots in between them.** String them in the following order: smoky topaz, pearl, light Colorado, pearl, light Colorado, pearl, black diamond pearl, black diamond, pearl, jet, pearl, jet, pearl, light Colorado, pearl, light Colorado, pearl, smoky topaz, pearl, smoky topaz. Tie a knot after your last crystal.

8. **Slide both strands of your cord through a bead tip. Make sure the mouth of the clamshell is pointing away from the bead strand. Tie two overhand knots. Add a dab of glue to the knot. Trim away the excess thread, and then close the clamshell over your knot, using your flat-nose pliers.**

9. **Using your round-nose pliers, attach one side of the toggle clasp to the loop of your bead tip.** Take a look at Figure 5-6 to see the best way to shape the loop using your pliers. Repeat with the second bead tip and the second piece of the clasp.

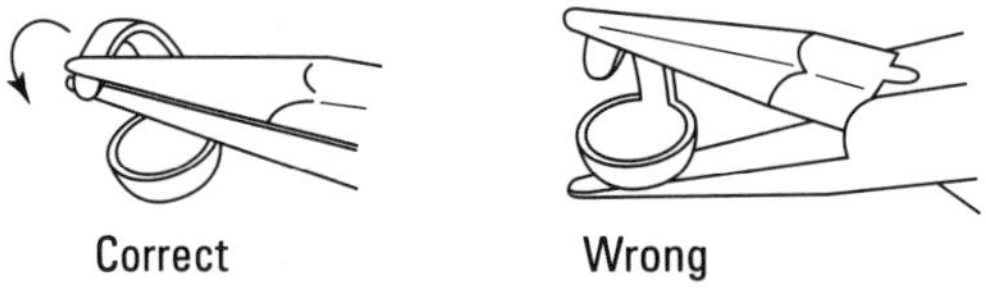

Figure 5-6:
Attaching bead tip loop with round-nose pliers.

Correct   Wrong

Figure 5-7:
Elegant Crystal and Freshwater Pearl Bracelet.

Knotting or Crimping: The End is Only the Beginning

Most of the time, I use two basic ways (with lots of variations, of course) to begin and end a piece of strand jewelry: by knotting it or by crimping it. Many jewelry designers prefer one or the other. Others take a more moderate approach, using both options as the design and materials dictate. I am in the latter category. I crimp, I knot, as it suits me.

A third option for beginning and ending strands exists. *Cord tips* are endings specifically made for wider cords. Some have a short tube on one end and an eye, hook, or other clasp end on the other. You put a dab of glue on your cord, insert it in the tube of the cord tip, and let them dry. Others require pliers to fold them into shape around your cord, sort of like a rough crimp. Take a look at Figure 5-8 to see a few styles of them.

Figure 5-8:
Cord tips are an easy way to end cord strands.

Using crimps

I use a crimp when I'm working with beading wire or cable. Crimps make a clean professional finish to your work. Crimping allows you to make a nice loop on the end to attach a clasp. Crimps are great for thicker threading materials that don't knot well.

Two kinds of crimp beads are available: tubes and rounds. The tube shaped crimp beads are most often available in sterling or gold-filled, while the round are normally made of base metal. In my opinion, crimp tubes are much easier to manage, especially when you're just starting out. The directions in the next section are the same whether you're using a crimp bead or tube.

Attaching a crimp

Take a close-up look at the nose of your crimp pliers. Hold them closed like the ones in Figure 5-9. You see two notches in the nose. The first is oval shaped, and the second is also oval but with a tiny arch in the middle of one side. Use each of these notches to create your crimp in two phases.

1. **Slip your crimp bead onto your beading wire.** Take the end of the wire and loop it back through the crimp bead, leaving a small amount of extra wire as a tail. Take a look at Figure 5-10a.

2. **Position the crimp bead and thread in the second oval of the pliers (the one with the dip), and close the pliers firmly around the bead.** You'll see the bead indent in the center and curl up on the sides. Check it out in Figure 5-10b for the front and side views.

3. **Move the crimp to the other oval of the pliers. Set the crimp on its side and close the pliers firmly again.** This step reshapes the crimp into a tube. Figure 5-10c shows you the front and side views of the finished crimp.

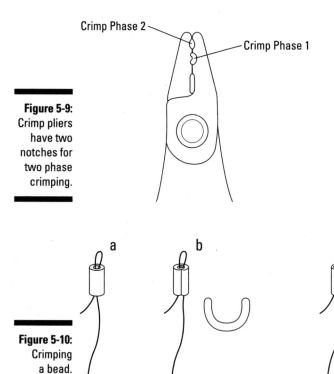

Crimp Phase 2

Crimp Phase 1

Figure 5-9:
Crimp pliers
have two
notches for
two phase
crimping.

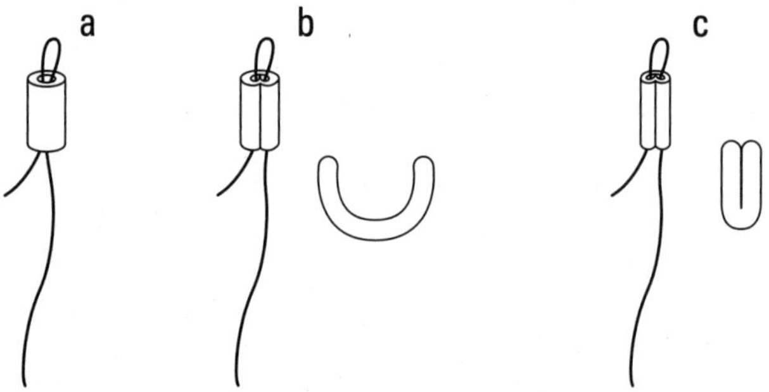

a   b   c

Figure 5-10:
Crimping
a bead.

This technique works for crimp pliers and micro-crimp pliers. *Micro-crimp pliers* are designed to work with 1×1mm crimp tubes and beads and smaller (0.01-inch diameter) beading wire. Use standard crimp pliers for 2×2mm beads and tubes and with standard beading wire diameters.

Definitely practice this technique until you like your results. It takes a several attempts to get it right. And definitely practice crimping the bead onto the wire, rather than just crimping an empty bead. It's much easier to move from the first phase to the second phase by holding onto the wire. Use the wire to keep the crimp on its side to finish the crimp properly.

Other crimping options

Many options are available to take crimping to the next level. Look for clasps with crimps already attached. Or use crimp tubes with loops to avoid looping your beading wire. Take a look at Figure 5-11 to see some other non-traditional crimping options.

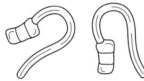

Figure 5-11: Crimping clasps terminate your strand in style.

Crimp pliers are optional, but I do recommend using them. If you're looking to cut your tool budget, you can use your flat-nosed pliers to flatten a crimp bead. The flattened crimp bead works the same way as a crimped crimp bead, but it doesn't look as pretty. The crimp pliers allow you to curl the bead tip, while the flat-nose pliers simply flatten it. For the most professional look, use crimp pliers and follow the steps in the preceding section.

Knot just the end, but the beginning, too

I use knots to finish and start strands when I'm working with elastic (sometimes), silk, or nylon bead cord, and smaller diameters (<1.0mm) of leather. Larger diameter cord (>2.0mm) usually calls for cord tips. Check out Chapter 2 for information on which cords knot well.

Some people use knotting and/or gluing only with elastic cord because they feel like the crimps can cut the elastic. While this can happen, I personally haven't had trouble with this. I carefully crimp elastic when I use it to make illusion-style necklaces like the one in Project 2-1 in Chapter 2, but I knot and glue stretch bracelets like the one in Project 5-1 in this chapter. Other people glue the beads on their illusion necklaces into place (instead of using crimps on either side of the beads). Try it both ways to see which you prefer.

Macramé jewelry is made up of a series of elaborate knots. Experienced macramé designers can incorporate beads and other components into their knotty designs for some truly beautiful effects. To try your hand at this technique, check out the basic Friendship Bracelet, Project 13-3 in Chapter 13.

You can find entire books on the subject of tying knots. Knots for fishing, knots for boating, knots for tying up prisoners, perhaps I've said too much. . . . Anyway, this section focuses on only a few basic knots, the ones commonly used in jewelry making.

For jewelry making, here's the list of knots I use most often and how I use them:

- ✔ **Overhand knot:** This knot is a super basic knot. Use it to tie knots inside bead tips. Take a look at it in Figure 5-12a. A double overhand knot is similar to an overhand knot, but you add another loop before you pull it tight, as shown in Figure 5-12b. The resulting knot is bulkier, which is exactly why you may consider using.

- ✔ **Slip knot:** A slipknot comes in handy when you want to knot the end of something while you're stringing it, but want to take it out easily later. Take a look at it in Figure 5-13 and use the following steps.

    1. **Start by tying an overhand knot like the one in Figure 5-12a.**

    2. **Before pulling the knot tight, thread the end back though the knot loop, as shown in Figure 5-13.**

    3. **Pull the knot tight, to finish.**

    Tie a variation of the slipknot on a cord twice to make an adjustable length cord. Here's how:

    1. **Lay both of the ends of your cord next to each other, pointed in opposite directions. See Figure 5-14a.**

    2. **Holding one strand stationary, tie a figure-eight around it with the other strand, as in Figure 5-14b.**

    3. **Slip the end of the strand used to make the figure-eight between the stationary strand and the figure-eight, as in Figure 5-14c.**

    4. **Pull the knot tight as shown in Figure 5-14d. Trim the excess cord from the loose end of the knot.**

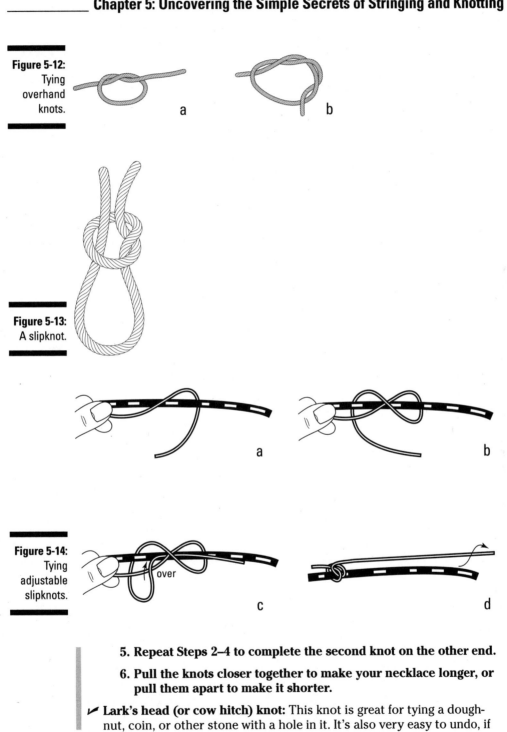

Figure 5-12:
Tying overhand knots.

Figure 5-13:
A slipknot.

Figure 5-14:
Tying adjustable slipknots.

5. Repeat Steps 2–4 to complete the second knot on the other end.

6. Pull the knots closer together to make your necklace longer, or pull them apart to make it shorter.

✔ **Lark's head (or cow hitch) knot:** This knot is great for tying a dough-nut, coin, or other stone with a hole in it. It's also very easy to undo, if necessary. Check out Figure 5-15 to see how this one works and follow these steps.

1. **Fold your cord in half. Thread the folded end through your doughnut, as shown in Figure 5-15a.**

2. **Pull the loop created by the folded end back up over the top of the doughnut. Take a look at Figure 5-15b.**

3. **Pull the loop tight to the cord to complete the knot as in Figure 5-15c.**

✔ **Square knot:** The square knot gets its name from the square shape the strands make before you tighten them down. Many people use this knot to finish stretch jewelry designs. I prefer to make an overhand knot with both ends of the cord together, because it holds much better. A square knot is a good choice for changing thread in the middle of a bead-weaving project.

1. **Cross both strands and twist them once, as shown in Figure 5-16a. Pull the ends apart.**

2. **Turn the ends back toward the middle. Cross the threads again and twist them again, to make a square like the one in Figure 5-16b. Pull them tight to complete the knot.**

Figure 5-15:
Use a lark's head knot to make a quick doughnut pendant.

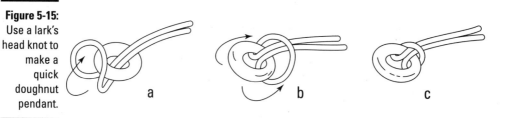

a   b   c

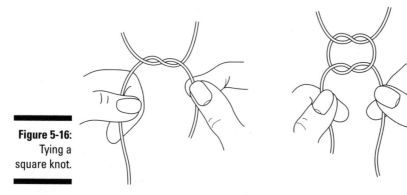

Figure 5-16:
Tying a square knot.

To Glue or Not to Glue

I glue knots when it's likely that they could come undone, especially at the end of a strand. I don't glue when I'm knotting in the middle of a piece, like when I'm knotting between beads in a strand.

The pros of gluing

Gluing keeps knots in place. But you better make sure a knot is where you want it, because if you're using glue suited for jewelry making, it dries fast and it will be nearly impossible to move it later.

The cons of gluing

This may be a good place to discuss the hazards of glues, needing to work in well-ventilated areas, and so on. E600, for example, is a great glue, used a lot for large items like gluing cabochons onto leather and such, but it is pretty toxic. Of course, most glues have warnings on them, but be sure to read the label of stuff like this. Also, some companies send information along with hazardous materials, such as glue, that they ship to you.

Keep in mind that when doing seed beading, glue can fill the hole in your beads, which you don't want. An alternative to glue for small knots that you just want to keep in place is clear fingernail polish.

Which glue for what?

People use many words to describe glues. You may hear the terms adhesive, sealant, cement, or even tackifier. For simplicity's sake, I'm calling them *glues* in this book. That moniker may not be completely accurate from a chemical formula standpoint, but for our use, it works.

You can find entire databases, books, and Web sites dedicated to glues and all their subtle differences. For simplicity's sake, I've included only glues that are clear-drying and used by the average jewelry maker.

> ✔ **Special-T illusion:** This glue is a great instant glue for jewelry making. It has a narrow tip giving you control to put your glue where you want it. It dries flexible, so it's a great choice for stretchy jewelry. Even though it's an instant glue, I still let it cure overnight before wearing or selling a piece.

✔ **Goop E600:** This adhesive agent is terrific for gluing just about anything, like gluing cabochons onto backing material, like leather, before adding beadwork. The tube is pretty large, though, so it's not a good choice for delicate work. Look for nozzles that screw on to give a little more accuracy.

✔ **Goop Crafter's adhesive:** This glue is a good choice for many crafting applications. I use it in Chapter 12 to add beaded fringe to a lamp shade. It's good to use in places where you won't see it because, although it dries clear, the texture of the dried glue can be a little rubbery.

✔ **Hypo-cement:** This product is a good choice for gluing small knots, half-drilled beads, and beads on illusion necklaces. The top has a long pin in it, designed to keep the glue free flowing, but it can be tough to get that pin back down the tube. It takes some practice to use, but it's a great product. It dries in about 10 minutes, but I let my pieces cure overnight. I use this glue for my stretch bracelets.

✔ **Instant bond glue:** You can find instant bond glue by several brand names, including Super glue, Krazy Glue, and QuickTite. It holds well and bonds instantly. But it doesn't give you very much control. It tends to go everywhere, including on your hands and workspace. It's probably a good choice for larger jewelry items, but not great for knots.

✔ **Instant gel adhesives:** These glues are very similar to instant bond glue, but they have a gel consistency, making them easier to get into and hold uneven surfaces together. Choose these for gluing odd-shaped beads to flat surfaces or for gluing broken pendants and cabochons when all edges may not match perfectly. Most instant bond glues offer a gel product, too.

✔ **Craft glue:** Look for brand names like Aleene's Tacky glue and Sobo Craft and Fabric glue. These craft glues dry to a clear, flexible finish. I use Aleene's Tacky Glue for gluing beads and rhinestones to things like the wooden picture frame in Chapter 12. Most craft glues are non-toxic, but they usually take awhile to dry.

✔ **Clear fingernail polish:** A good choice for small, delicate jobs. It won't hold well in high stress applications. It can flake off. It's extremely easy to use, and you probably already have it in your home.

No matter which glue you choose for which project, always read the instructions before you use it. (The time to know what to do if you glue your fingers together is before you glue your fingers together.) You need to know how to use it properly and get safety precaution information. Look for information on what to do if your skin or eyes come into contact with the product. Get the details on ventilation requirements, because most adhesive products are toxic to some degree.

Chapter 6

Discovering the Ancient Art of Bead Weaving

. . . .

In This Chapter

▶ Getting it together for bead weaving

▶ Identifying bead weaving stitches

. . . .

*B*ead weaving is a term that describes the process of combining beads in a strand by interlacing thread through the beads. In most cases, designers weave seed beads and bugle beads to create delicate, intricate designs. They also incorporate other beads as accents on occasion. The Teardrop Seed Bead Necklace (Project 6-3), for example, is made up primarily of seed beads, but also uses larger 4mm beads and 10 × 8mm faceted teardrop beads as accent beads. Sometimes this style of bead weaving is called *off-loom weaving,* because it doesn't require a loom.

In this chapter, I give you the basics of off-loom bead weaving. I show you what you need to get started. I provide some general tips for successful bead weaving. Then, I introduce you to several basic bead weaving stitches and give you tips on using them to develop your own projects and designs.

Gathering Materials for Bead Weaving

Bead weaving requires a few different tools in addition to the standard jewelry-making gear identified in Chapter 2. Depending on how you want to wear your pieces, you may need clasps, earring findings, and the like.

Here's a quick list of materials needed specifically for bead weaving:

✔ **Thread:** Most bead weaving pieces use Nymo or Silamide thread. *Nymo* is made of nylon, is not waxed, and is slightly twisted; *Silamide* is similar, but it comes pre-waxed. Depending on how your piece is to be worn, elastic or stretchy cord may also be a good choice. I often use the stretchy cord for bracelets, headbands, and toe rings.

✔ **Thread conditioner:** For many pieces, you'll begin working with a long thread, so you won't need to change or add thread in the middle of a piece. Use thread conditioner to keep your thread from tangling and knotting. Many people use beeswax or a product called Thread Heaven for this purpose. Thread conditioner also helps to keep sharper beads from cutting your cord.

✔ **Beading needles:** Because you're working with thread, a beading needle is essential to the weaving process. They come in sizes 10 through 16. The larger the number, the thinner the needle. They basically correspond to the seed bead sizes: the higher the number, the smaller the seed bead.

✔ **Scissors:** Get a small pair of sharp scissors, like embroidery or sewing scissors, to cut your fine thread cleanly. As silly as it may sound, when I first started, I though I could cut my thread with my wire cutters. Well, needless to say, they do cut thread, but they don't do it well. They leave your ends frayed and rough. Not pretty. Invest in some small, sharp scissors to keep your ends clean.

✔ **Work mat:** For working with tiny beads, choose a work mat (also called a *work* pad) made from a nappy fiber like felt, velvet, or fleece. This material helps minimize the bead chase scenes during your beading.

✔ **Beads:** In most cases, bead-weaving techniques use seed beads and bugle beads in a variety of sizes. For more about beads, check out Chapter 3.

Project 6-1: Flower Seed Bead Bracelet

This bracelet is a great project to begin to get used to picking up beads with your needle, forming shapes with your strands of beads, and rethreading your needle through a bead multiple times. Plus, it's really cute. To see the final product, check out Figure 6-3.

Tools and Materials

Scissors

Hypo-cement (or clear fingernail polish)

Corsage pin, beading awl, or tweezers

Flat-nose pliers

Size 10 beading needle

5 feet, size "A" purple Silamide or Nymo thread

2 gold-tone bead tips

1 gold-tone jump ring

1 gold-tone spring ring clasp

48 size 11 green seed beads (these form the leaves of the flower pattern)

220 size 11 purple seed beads (these form the petals of the flower pattern)

5 4mm yellow glass beads (these are the centers of the flowers)

2 extra size 11 seed beads, any color

1. **Thread your needle with the Silamide thread. Double the thread and knot it at the end.**

2. **Slide one of your extra seed beads onto your thread and push it down against the knot. Loop the thread around the bead and thread the needle through the bead again. As you pull the thread through the bead, make sure the bead is at the very end of your thread. You're using the bead as an extra security measure.** Take a look at Figure 6-1a.

3. **Thread the bead tip onto your thread so that the extra bead rests inside the clamshell of the bead tip.** Add a dab of Hypo-cement to your extra bead and knot, and then use your pliers to close the shell around the bead, as shown in Figure 6-1b.

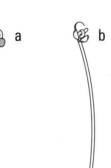

Figure 6-1:
Adding a
seed bead
to your
bead tip
adds extra
security to
your knot.

4. **Using your needle,** *pick up,* **or slide onto your thread, two green beads, two purple beads, and two more green beads. Loop the beads around in a counterclockwise circle and thread your needle through the first 2 green beads again.** It should look like Figure 6-2a. Continue rethreading through the two purple beads.

5. **Pick up 6 purple beads, 1 yellow bead, and 6 more purple beads. Create a loop by moving the strand in a clockwise motion and rethreading through the original 2 purple beads.** Take a look at Figure 6-2b for help.

6. **Continue moving your needle through the loop in a clockwise direction until you have gone through three purple beads past the yellow bead. Pick up 11 purple beads. Making a counterclockwise motion, form a loop and rethread through the center yellow bead. Continue counterclockwise through the 3 purple beads next to the yellow bead.** You've created your second petal. It should look like the one in Figure 6-2c.

7. **Pick up 11 more purple beads and loop them clockwise, through the center yellow bead. Continue through the 3 purple beads below and to the right of the yellow bead. Pick up 8 more purple beads and loop them counterclockwise.** Rethread them through the 3 purple beads

before the center (above and to the right of the yellow center bead), and then through the yellow center bead to create the final loop as shown in Figure 6-2d.

8. **Continue threading down through the yellow center bead, through the 3 beads that are common to the bottom loop and your new loop, and finally up through the first 5 beads of your new loop.** Your thread should now be coming out of the bead one up from the middle of the last loop you created.

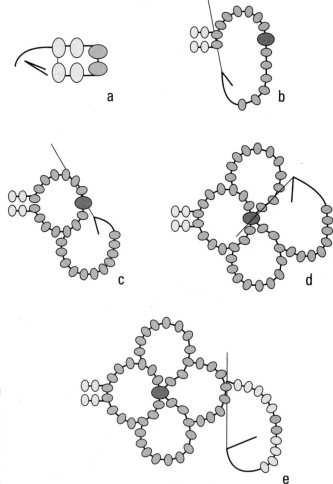

Figure 6-2:
Steps to complete a seed bead flower.

9. **Pick up 5 green beads, 2 purple beads, and 5 more green beads.** (These beads form the leaves between the flowers and the beginning of the next flower petal.) Make a loop, going clockwise and thread up through the bead below the bead your thread is coming out of. Take a look at Figure 6-2e. Rethread through the first 5 stem beads and the 2 flower beads and you are ready to start your next flower!

10. **Repeat Steps 5–8 to complete 4 additional flowers, each separated by leaves (for a total of 5 flowers and 4 leaves).** After you've completed your last flower pick up 2 green beads, 2 purple beads, and 2 green beads (instead of 5 green, 2 purple, 5 green used between the flowers). This step ensures that your end will match your beginning.

11. **With your needle, pick up your last clamshell bead tip. Pick up your last extra bead. Use a corsage pin (or beading awl or tweezers) to tie and push your knot and seed bead into your bead tip.** For help with traditional knotting, take a look at Chapter 5. Apply a little dab of glue. Cut the thread close to the knot. Close the bead tip with your pliers.

12. **Attach the bead tip to your jump ring and the other to the springring clasp.**

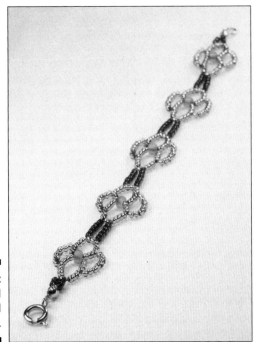

Figure 6-3:
Flower Seed
Bead
Bracelet.

Choosing the Right Stitch for Your Design

A *stitch* in bead weaving is the pattern of beads and threads you use to create your designs. Many pieces employ multiple stitches to get a wide variety of colors, textures, and eye appealing transitions. Take a look at this section for information on how to do these basic stitches and look for ideas to help you incorporate them into your own pieces.

Daisy stitch

The *daisy stitch* is one of the most recognizable bead weaving stitches, because the finished stitch looks like, well, a daisy. You can play up the daisy design by choosing consistent petal and center colors throughout your piece. Or, you can use the stitch, but ignore the traditional color-coding to come up with more sophisticated designs.

I like to make daisy stitch headbands and bracelets using clear stretchy cord.

Here are the basic steps for completing the daisy stitch:

1. **Thread your needle with your choice of thread. Pick up 4 petal color beads and one center color bead. Moving counter clockwise, begin to create a loop. Thread your needle back through the first petal bead.** Take a look at Figure 6-4a to see how this works.

Figure 6-4: Creating a daisy chain.

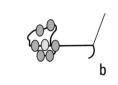

a   b   c

2. **Now add 2 more petal beads.** Thread your needle through the petal bead on the far side of your center bead, as shown in Figure 6-4b.

3. **Continue adding daisies until your piece reaches your desired length.** Figure 6-4c shows several daisies connected.

Choose smaller seed beads for more delicate daisies and larger for a more adolescent look. Kids can even make this stitch using plastic bead cord and pony beads. For large beads, omit the needle, of course!

Your 6-inch tail is good for a few things, depending on what you're making. Use it to finish your piece off by knotting it or reinserting through beads to shore up your structure. It's also helpful in the event that you make a mistake and need to unravel some of what you've done.

Ladder stitch

The *ladder stitch* is a base for many bead weaving projects. It's most often created with bugle beads, but can also be created with multiple seed beads, serving as "rungs," as I do in this section.

In order to be a ladder stitch, the thread can pass only through the ends of the rungs, never through the middle of the rungs, even if you're using several seed beads per rung.

Here are the steps to create a basic seed bead ladder:

1. **Thread a beading needle with a single strand of thread. Slide on 6 seed beads and push them down toward the end of the unknotted thread. Leave a 6-inch tail.** Take a look at Figure 6-5a.

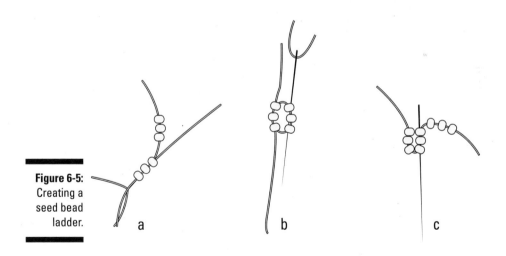

Figure 6-5: Creating a seed bead ladder.

a   b   c

2. **Insert the needle through the first 3 seed beads added in Step 1. Pull the needle and thread taut (hanging onto to the tail) until the two sets of 3 beads are side by side.** Thread your needle down through the second set of beads, as shown in Figure 6-5b.

3. **Pick up 3 more beads. Slide the third set of beads to the end of the thread. Pass the needle and thread back around through the second set of beads.** For help see Figure 6-5c. Continue adding beads until your ladder is long enough for your project.

4. **Weave your needle and thread back through the beads to reinforce your ladder.**

This stitch is a great beginner stitch. Use elastic cord to make a ladder stitch stretchy bracelet in a snap. Or create several ladders, and then weave them together to make a purse. For more practice, try making the fringe earrings in Project 6-2.

Hold on tight to your ladder the whole time you're weaving it. Otherwise, you'll have gaps and pulls and a poor finished project. If you do have trouble, try threading your needle back through all of the beads in your ladder stitch. You may be able to shape it up a bit this way.

Brick stitch

The *brick stitch* is another basic stitch in bead weaving. It gets its name from its final appearance that resembles a brick wall, with one bead stacked on top of two beads where the two beads meet. Before you start a brick stitch, you need a base to build on, because you actually attach the beads to the thread that connects two other beads. Most people build a brick stitch on top of a ladder stitch.

Here are the basic steps to create a brick stitch:

1. **Start with a bugle bead ladder. Bring your needle up through the first bugle bead on one end of the ladder. Make sure you leave a 6-inch tail.**

Make a bugle bead ladder by following the steps in the "Ladders stitch" section earlier in this chapter, but make your "rungs" from a single bugle bead rather than 3 seed beads.

2. **Thread on one seed bead. Insert your needle under the thread that joins the first two rungs and wrap is over,** as shown in Figure 6-6a.

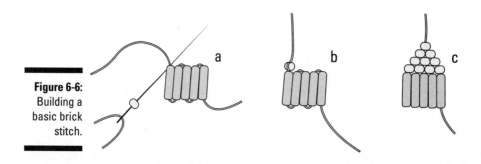

Figure 6-6: Building a basic brick stitch.

3. **Insert your needle up through the bead hole of the bead you added in Step 2. Push the bead down so that it sits snuggly against the top of the ladder.** Take a look at Figure 6-6b for help.

4. **Repeat Steps 2 and 3 until you've worked your way across the length of your ladder.**

5. **When you get to the end of the row, flip your piece over to begin the row, so you can continue working left to right. As you do each row, the length of each row will automatically be one bead shorter than the previous row.** If you continue doing row after row, you end up with a piece shaped like a triangle. Check out Figure 6-6c.

6. **If you want to create a squared-off brick stitch pattern (instead of a triangular pattern), pick up another seed bead when you get to the end of a row. Run your needle and thread down the bead sitting next to it (which would have been your last bead, if you'd stuck with the triangle), and then back again through the newly added bead.** Continue adding your new row on top.

You may also hear the brick stitch referred to as *Comanche weave.* Just another term for the same basic stitch.

Project 6-2: Fringe Earrings

These earrings are quick to work up, giving you a quick sense of accomplishment. Use the basic ladder and brick stitches to get them started. Then add beautiful dangles for an elegant look. Take a look at the finished project in Figure 6-9.

Tools and Materials

Scissors

Round-nose pliers

Beading needle, size 10

Corsage pin, beading awl, or tweezers

20¼-inch Japanese bugle beads, purple rainbow

62 size 11 Japanese seed beads, dark amethyst rainbow

3 feet Nymo or Silamide thread size A, off-white

10 side drilled teardrop beads, champagne

2 ear hooks

Thread conditioner

1. **Thread your needle. Using 5 bugle beads, create a ladder base. Use the ladder stitch (refer to Figure 6-5) to create the first part of the earrings.** Remember to keep a 6-inch tail of thread and to hold the bugles with your fingers as you stitch in order to keep gaps to a minimum. Your ladder should look like the one in Figure 6-7a.

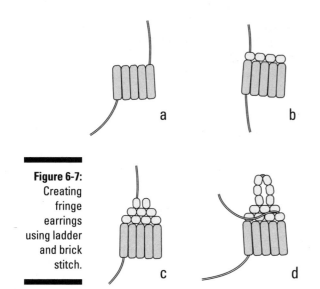

Figure 6-7:
Creating
fringe
earrings
using ladder
and brick
stitch.

2. **With your thread coming out of the top of the last bugle bead you connected to your ladder, do a row of brick stitch across the ladder, using 4 seed beads.** When your row is complete, it looks like Figure 6-7b.

3. **Continue doing brick back and forth across the top of the ladder for two more rows.** The length rows will automatically decrease until you have a triangle at the top, and will end with 2 seed beads in your last row, as in Figure 6-7c.

4. **Now, you're ready to make a loop at the top that your ear hook will go through. Pick up 4 seed beads and go down through the seed bead next to the bead your thread is coming out of as shown in Figure 6-7d.**

Because the ear hooks will be attached to this loop, you want to be sure it is very secure. Bring the needle up and down a few times through the beads to make it nice and secure. Finish this by coming down through the beads until you come out of the center bugle. Check out Figure 6-8a to see what this looks like.

5. **Pick up 3 seed beads, 1 bugle bead, 3 more seed beads, and one teardrop. The project should look like Figure 6-8b. Bring your needle up through the 3 seed beads, the bugle bead, and the 3 seed beads.** (Your thread will go around the teardrop bead, which then forms the end of the dangle.) Continue going up through the middle bugle in your ladder so the fringe is in the center of the bugle ladder and the teardrop bead is at the end of your first piece of fringe.

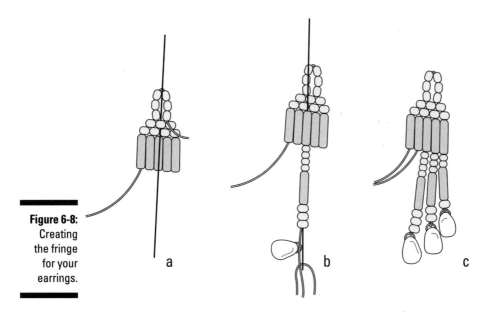

Figure 6-8:
Creating
the fringe
for your
earrings.

a   b   c

Don't pull too tightly on your fringe, or the side-drilled teardrop may end
up sideways instead of straight up and down. Adjust the fringe, as necessary, as you work to keep the teardrops hanging straight.

6. **Go down through the next bugle bead (to the right of the center bugle
   bead) to add the next piece of fringe.**

   You can work to the right or to the left depending on your preference.
   Just reverse the "right" and "left" in the instructions. Note, though, that
   the Figure 6-8c shows the project proceeding from the center to the right.

7. **Pick up 2 seed beads, 1 bugle, 2 seed beads, and one teardrop. Repeat
   the rest of Step 5, but this time finish the fringe by coming up through
   the bugle bead to the right of center bugle bead.**

8. **Repeat Step 5, but use 1 seed bead, 1 bugle, 1 seed bead, and 1 teardrop, and finish the fringe by coming up the end bugle bead on the
   right.**

9. **Thread your needle through the bugle bead ladder until your thread
   is coming down out of the bugle to the left of the middle bugle bead,
   as shown in Figure 6-8c.**

10. **Repeat Step 6, but finish the fringe by coming up through the bugle
    bead to the left of center bugle bead.** Repeat Step 7, but finish the
    fringe by coming up the end bugle bead on the left.

Figure 6-9:
Fringe
Earrings.

11. **Finish this earring by threading the leftover thread through beads. Make a small overhand knot before slipping the thread through more beads and clipping it off. Do the same with your tail.**

12. **Use round-nose pliers to open the loop in your ear hook. Slip on the beaded loop at the top of your earring into the loop of the hook, and use round-nose pliers to close the ear hook loop.**

13. **Repeat Steps 1 through 11 to create a matching earring so you have a pair.**

Peyote stitch

You can find many different variations of what's called *peyote stitch*. Some versions make a tube; others are flat. Some use an even number of beads in the first row; others use an odd number. Other people use the stitch, but call it by different names, like the twill stitch. Whatever you call it, it's a great stitch to learn to add additional detail to your bead weaving projects.

When you're first learning this stitch, use two contrasting color beads. It will help you keep your place and reveal the full design of the stitch.

Here's how to do a basic flat peyote stitch:

1. **Tie a black bead to the end of your thread and go back through it once. Now pick up 9 beads, alternating between white and black beads.** This completes your first row, as seen in Figure 6-10a.

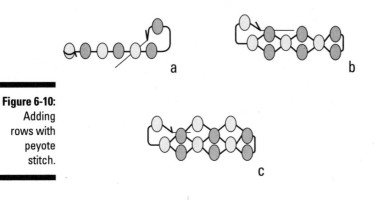

Figure 6-10:
Adding
rows with
peyote
stitch.

2. **Pick up a white bead.** *Tie on,* or thread, **your needle through the black bead from the first row. Pick up another white bead. Tie on through the next black bead. Continue this process until you reach the end of the row. You should start to see a zigzag pattern developing as the second row of white beads push the first row down.** Take a look at Figure 6-10b.

When you're doing the peyote stitch, the white beads you just added are considered one row, but are actually the third row, to be precise. The base row is considered two rows, because it splits into two rows, one black (Row 2) and one white (Row 1).

3. **After you've completed Row 3, add Row 4. Pick up a black bead. Tie on a white bead. Pick up a black bead, and then tie on another white bead.** Continue until you reach the end of the row, just like in Figure 6-10c.

4. **Continue adding rows until you've reached your desired length.**

The peyote stitch is great for creating cuff bracelets, covering small bags or bottles, or making belts.

Net stitch

The *net stitch* is a quick way to cover a lot of space using beads. Make great collar necklaces with this stitch or cool fringe for a lamp, valance, or other home décor item (see Chapter 12).

Here are the steps to create a basic net stitch:

1. **Pick up beads in the following pattern: 1 black bead, 3 white beads. Repeat three times. Pick up 1 additional black bead. The black beads will be the *anchor beads,* meaning that each time you add a new row, you'll tie it in through this point, in the net stitch. Make sure to leave a 6-inch tail.** Your strand should look something like Figure 6-11a.

2. **Pick up a white bead, a black bead, and a white bead. Thread your needle through the closest black anchor bead in the first row. (In this example, I am working from right to left for the first row of swags.) Continue repeating this pattern until you've created "swags" to connect all the beads in the first row.** Take a look at Figure 6-11b.

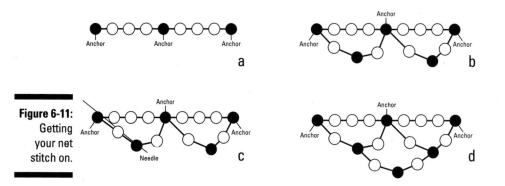

Figure 6-11:
Getting
your net
stitch on.

3. **Now *step down,* or begin working on the next row below, by threading your needle around and back through the black bead in the first row.** Thread your needle through the white bead in the swag and the new black anchor bead, as shown in Figure 6-11c.

4. **Repeat Step 2, working your way across he necklace from left to right, as in Figure 6-11d.** Continue making swags and stepping down until your piece is complete.

You can continue to add rows or tie off your necklace and then add dangles at the anchor beads in the last row. To try your hand at a little bit of netting, check out Project 6-3 to create a Teardrop Seed Bead Necklace.

Project 6-3: Teardrop Seed Bead Necklace

This project uses basic steps from the net stitch. But because it has a single seed bead cord, you can make it very quickly. Vary your colors to match a favorite outfit or celebrate a holiday. Take a look at Figure 6-14 to see the finished project.

Tools and Materials

Size 10 beading needle	2 extra seed beads, size 11, any color
Flat-nose pliers	2 sterling bead tips
Corsage pin, beading awl, or tweezers	1 sterling jump ring
Scissors	1 sterling spring ring clasp
10 grams (or about 350) size 11 white seed beads	Size "A" cream-colored Silamide or Nymo thread
7 10x8mm sapphire-colored Czech crystal teardrop beads	Hypo-cement (or clear fingernail polish)
14 4mm AB light blue Czech crystal bicone beads	Thread conditioner

1. **Thread your needle with the thread. Double the thread and knot the end.** Condition it thoroughly according to the manufacturers directions beforehand, so that it will slide easily and resist knots.

2. **Slide one of your extra seed beads onto your thread and push it down against the knot. Loop the thread around the bead and thread the needle through the bead again.** As you pull the thread through the bead, make sure the bead is at the very end of your thread. You're using the bead as an extra security. Refer to Figure 6-1a to see how this works.

3. **Thread the bead tip onto your thread so that the extra bead rests inside the clamshell of the bead tip. Add a dab of Hypo-cement to your extra bead and knot, and then use your pliers to close the shell around the bead;** refer to Figure 6-1b.

4. **Pick up 100 seed beads, and then one 4mm bead, and follow it with 10 seed beads.** Continue alternating between one 4mm bead and 10 seed beads until you have strung on 8 of the 4mm beads and 7 sections of 10 seed beads. Finish the strand by picking up 100 white seed beads.

5. **With your needle, pick up your last clamshell bead tip. Pick up your last extra bead. Use a corsage pin (or beading awl or tweezers) to tie and push your knot and seed bead into your bead tip.** For help with traditional knotting, take a look at Chapter 5. Apply a little dab of glue. Cut the thread close to the knot. Close the bead tip with your pliers. Attach 1 bead tip to your jump ring and the other to the springring clasp.

In Step 6, you're going to reattach your needle and thread to the necklace. If necessary, rethread your needle with more thread, but for the rest of the necklace, you don't need to use a double thickness of thread.

6. **A few inches from your last 4mm bead, insert the needle through some of the seed beads on your necklace and leave about a 4-inch tail of thread. With your new thread, tie a knot around the thread that you originally used to string your necklace.** If desired, dab a dot of glue onto

the knot. Your seed beads will cover the knot. Repeat this step securing another knot onto your first thread.

7. **Continue to thread the needle through the seed beads and bring the needle out after going through the 4mm bead. Pick up 10 seed beads, one teardrop bead, and one seed bead. Bring the needle back up through the bottom of the teardrop bead, and pull the thread to push the beads together.** Check out Figure 6-12 for help. One seed bead rests under the teardrop bead, holding it in place. String on 10 more seed beads, and then thread the needle through the next 4mm bead.

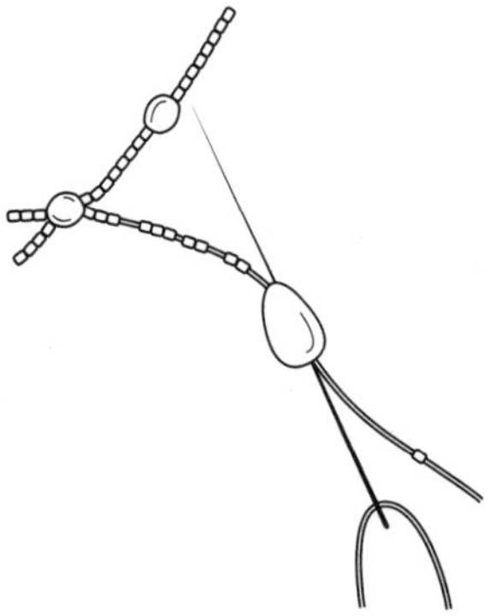

Figure 6-12:
Adding a net stitch element to your necklace.

8. **Repeat Step 7 until you have used up all the teardrop beads.** You should have 7 triangle pieces hanging from your necklace.

9. **To make the connecting row of beads and crystals, insert your needle through the last three seed beads past your last 4mm bead. Bring your needle up through the bottom of the last seed bead you just brought your needle through, tying an overhand knot around the seed bead. Then skip this bead and go back through the other beads (the two seed beads and 4mm bead from Step 8) until you come out of the same 4mm bead, but now you'll be going in the opposite direction.** Take a look at Figure 6-13a to see how this works.

10. **Thread your way through any of the seed beads so that you position your needle to come out of the fifth seed bead on the inside of your last triangle teardrop section as shown in Figure 6-13b.**

11. **Slide on 2 seed beads, 1 4mm bead, and 2 more seed beads, and insert the needle back through the fifth seed bead on the next teardrop triangle section.** Check out Figure 6-13c if you need help. Continue this process (working around each triangle) until you have connected all of the triangle sections.

12. **Finish off the thread by knotting as you did in Step 6, trim off excess threads as necessary, and if desired, dab a very tiny bit of glue onto any of the knots you've made.**

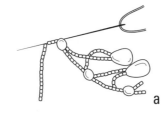

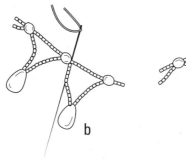

Figure 6-13:
Connecting
the triangles
with beads.

Figure 6-14:
Teardrop
Seed Bead
Necklace.

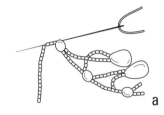

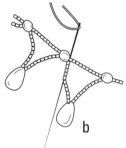

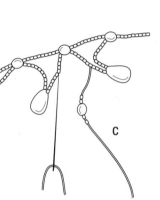

Figure 6-13:
Connecting
the triangles
with beads.

a

b

c

Figure 6-14:
Teardrop
Seed Bead
Necklace.

Chapter 7

Winding It Up with Wire Wrapping

Working with wire provides endless design possibilities for jewelry making. By wrapping wire by itself, or intertwining it with beads, you can create beautiful wire-wrapped jewelry components. From simple memory wire designs to beaded rosary-style links used in necklaces to freeform shapes used in pendants to Victorian-inspired curved filigree used in clasps and earrings to modern, eclectic twists used for everything from brooches to bracelets, you can never stop learning enough about this exciting jewelry-making technique. You can find entire books on the subject.

In this chapter, I introduce you to the basics of wire wrapping, including helping you choose the right wire and technique for your project. I provide some fun projects to get you started, and I hope to inspire you to develop your own ideas. And I show you how to create a custom clasp to finish off your original design.

Choosing the Right Wire for the Job

Wire is an excellent addition to any jewelry maker's toolbox. Get started with memory wire to make a choker or bracelet in minutes, and then expand your supply closet to include bendable, wrappable wire in your creations.

Using memory wire

Memory wire is rigid, precoiled wire that holds its shape and strings very easily. Check out Chapter 2 for details on the sizes available. It's a great way to get started working with beads and wire together in a design.

Because memory wire is rigid and will retain its shape even while you wear it, you don't need to add a clasp.

If you're going to use memory wire very often, use memory wire shears instead of regular wire cutters. Cutting memory wire with regular cutters will damage them over time.

Project 7-1: Hematite Crystal Choker

With this design, you can create a stunning necklace in about 30 minutes. (***Note:*** I recommend that you let the glue cure overnight before wearing it.) I use hematite (one of my very favorite semi-precious stones) because I love the shine, especially when paired with the crystals. Use this choker to dress up any casual outfit or complement a trendy cocktail dress. Check out Figure 7-1 to take a look at the finished project.

Tools and Materials

1¼ coils necklace memory wire (standard size)

112 2x2mm hematite tubes

17 5mm clear crystal faceted rounds, AB finish

2 silver end caps

Glue (Superglue or Special-T glue)

1. **Put a small dab of glue on the silver end cap. Insert one end of the memory wire into end cap.** Allow glue to dry for 5 or 10 minutes.

2. **String one crystal onto other end of the memory wire. Add 7 hematite beads. Add another crystal.**

3. **Repeat Step 2 until all the beads are used. Note that your last bead should be a crystal.** You should have about ⅛-inch of memory wire left. If you have more, trim away the excess. Repeat Step 1 with the last end cap.

If you prefer, you can skip the glue and end caps and, instead, just make a small loop at each end of the memory wire to keep the beads from falling off. Just make sure to use about 1½ coils of memory wire (instead of the 1¼ listed in the directions) so you'll have enough to loop. If you use this tip with other designs, put larger beads (at least 3mm) next to the loops.

Figure 7-1:
Stunning
Hematite
Crystal
Choker.

Wire for wrapping

I've seen just about every kind of wire used in jewelry making, including wire intended for industrial and commercial uses, like that in your computer or in the electrical circuitry of your home. Anything that twists and holds the shape you give it can work for wire-wrapped jewelry. But in this chapter, I focus on the most commonly used wire for wire-wrapped jewelry. Check out Chapter 2 for details on how the wires differ.

Precious metal wire is used for wire wrapping, chain making, and other jewelry applications, like creating findings. It's available in several metals including platinum, gold-filled, and sterling silver, in three shapes (round, half-round, and square), and in three hardnesses (dead soft, half-hard, and full-hard). You can even buy it already twisted. Look for brass, copper, and niobium-based wire available in various colors and widths as well.

The more you bend precious metal wire, the more brittle it becomes, so be careful.

Like cord, leather, and thread, wire comes in several weights and widths, called *gauges.* As a rule, the higher the gauge, the thinner and softer the wire. For example, 22-gauge is thicker than 26-gauge.

 Start out with several gauges of copper or brass practice wire. It's much less expensive than silver or gold wire, is available at most hardware stores for only a few dollars, and is a great way to help you learn wire work. Even now, I use it when I work on a new technique or design.

Here's a quick rundown on the different precious metal wire hardnesses and what to use them for.

- **Dead soft wire** is extremely *malleable,* which means it can be bent easily into shapes. Because it's so easily bent, it doesn't hold its shape when pulled or tugged, so it's not a good choice for making clasps, jump rings, or other findings. Use it for making decorative shapes in earrings and bar-rettes. Bend the wire easily with your hands or use tools, if you prefer.

- **Half-hard wire** is malleable and will maintain its shape under some stress. Use it to create wire loops for rosary-style bead links or for earwires for lighter earrings. Choose this hardness for wrapping light beads or making scroll designs like in Project 7-2 later in this chapter. You can bend the lighter gauges easily with your hands, but may need tools for the heavier gauges of half hard wire.

- **Full-hard wire** is the least malleable wire, but it holds its shape much better than the other hardnesses. Use it for wire wrapping, especially in situations that you need the wire to hold its shape like for a clasp. You may need pliers and/or a *jig,* a board with pegs to wrap wire around, to help you bend the wire into specific shapes. Check out the "Gettin' Jiggy with It: Wire Jig Projects" section later in this chapter for details on working with a jig.

 Because precious metal wire can tarnish over time, polish the wire and your finished jewelry creations gently with a polishing cloth. Look for them at most jewelry supply stores, online catalogs, or even at stores like Wal-Mart or Target. Silver is a more active metal than gold, meaning it tends to tarnish faster. So silver designs need more polishing to keep them shiny and new. Of course, if you prefer an antique look, you can skip the polishing and keep the tarnish.

Deciphering wire shapes and sizes

To understand what the shape of a wire means, imagine that you cut the wire and look at the cut end head on. A wire can be *round* (the end looks like a full circle), *square* (the end looks like a square), or *half-round* (the end looks like a semi-circle, round on one side, flat on the other). Take a look at Figure 7-2 for an example of each of the shapes and gauges of round and square wire. While the shape of wire you choose depends on your preference and specific design, I like to use the round mostly for making loops, earwires, and twists. Square and half-round wire are good for wrapping around cabochons or other flat-sided beads, but it is just a matter of preference. You can use 6.5mm wide heavier gauge flat or half-round wire for cuff bracelets (but you'll need to file and sand the ends to smooth them down).

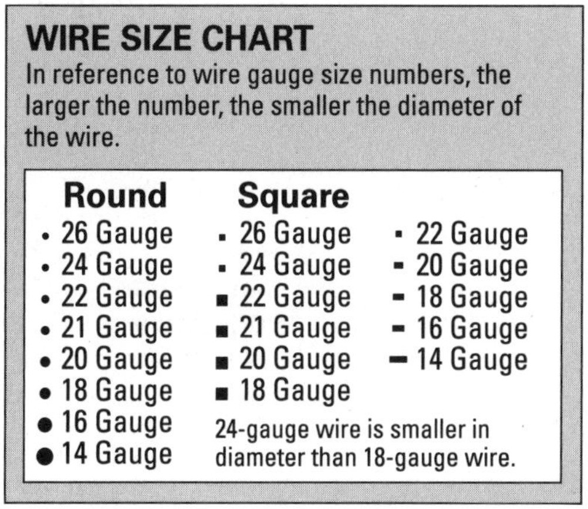

Figure 7-2:
Various wire shapes and sizes.

WIRE SIZE CHART

In reference to wire gauge size numbers, the larger the number, the smaller the diameter of the wire.

Round	Square	
• 26 Gauge	▪ 26 Gauge	▪ 22 Gauge
• 24 Gauge	▪ 24 Gauge	▪ 20 Gauge
• 22 Gauge	▪ 22 Gauge	▪ 18 Gauge
• 21 Gauge	▪ 21 Gauge	▪ 16 Gauge
• 20 Gauge	▪ 20 Gauge	▬ 14 Gauge
• 18 Gauge	▪ 18 Gauge	
• 16 Gauge		
● 14 Gauge		

24-gauge wire is smaller in diameter than 18-gauge wire.

Fire Mountain Gems and Beads™
(www.firemoutaingems.com/fordummies)

Here's a list of my recommendations for wire for different jewelry-making projects:

✔ For making bead links, I recommend using 22- or 24-gauge wire.

✔ For making medium weight drops or dangles, use 22-gauge wire.

✔ For delicate beadwork, like winding beads around a barrette or hairpin, use 26-gauge.

✔ For making clasps and earwires, I suggest using 21- or 22-gauge wire, round or twisted. If you use a higher gauge, the wearer will have trouble fitting it through her ear hole.

✔ For very delicate designs with tiny beads, use super-fine 32-gauge wire.

✔ For making loops and intricate molded designs, use 20- or 22-gauge wire.

When you're using bead and wire together, consider the size of your bead hole when you're choosing the gauge of the wire to use.

Identifying optional wire-wrapping tools

Nylon jaw pliers not only help protect wire from nicks and scratches, but they also help straighten out wire without denting it. (Check out Chapter 2 for a picture of these pliers.) In case you mess up a loop or something (which happens, believe me), simply use this handy tool to unbend the wire and straighten it by pressing it with the nose of the pliers. Straightening your wire this way saves you from wasting wire!

But don't waste your time straightening your practice wire. If you mess up, simply throw it out and start over again. It's cheap, which is why you practice with it.

If you need to wrap several wire pieces together, consider buying rubber-coated clamps or clips. Check out Figure 7-3 to see these. They're like a pair of extra hands to hold your design together while you secure it with wire. Look for them at jewelry supply stores or Web sites. Alternatively, you can also use binder clips available at most office supply stores. Just add a little bit of electrical tape to cushion the wire a bit and minimize scratching.

Figure 7-3:
Rubber-
coated
clamps hold
wire-
wrapping
projects in
place.

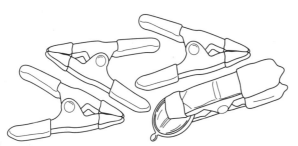

Bent-nose pliers are similar to long-nose pliers but with a slightly rounded or bent tip — great to making loops and reaching small places, and wrapping thin wire. You can get a close-up view of these pliers in Chapter 2.

Jewelry files help file down the sharp edges left when you cut wire. Using a jewelry file helps keep your wire creations from poking the wearer. Even though these tools look a bit like fingernail files, they definitely aren't. So invest in a set (they cost around $10) and don't experiment with your comparatively soft fingernail file.

Getting Familiar with Wrapping Techniques

Before you create the next award-winning wire design that will have the crowds lining up at Tiffany's, you need to first master a few basic techniques. Remember to play with your practice wire and get comfortable with the pliers. Don't waste the expensive stuff at this point!

Start with a simple zigzag:

1. **Cut about 6 inches of 24-gauge practice wire.**

2. **Take your flat-nose pliers in one hand and the piece of wire in the other hand. Bend the wire into a zigzag shape** as shown in Figure 7-4. Don't worry if it looks uneven; you're just practicing. Keep going until you feel confident that the zigs and the zags start looking similar.

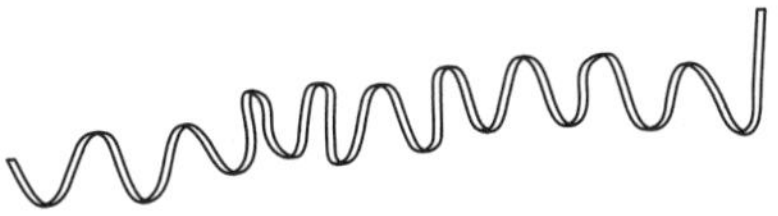

Figure 7-4:
Wire
zigzags.

After you've mastered the zigzag, try an *"S" scroll:*

1. **Cut about 6 inches of 24-gauge practice wire.**

2. **Take your round-nose pliers in one hand and insert the tip of the wire into the jaws of the pliers with the other hand. Slowly begin to wrap the wire around the tip of the pliers, gradually expanding the wire.** See Figure 7-5a (think expanding spirals or droplets of water).

3. **Do the same thing at the other end of the wire, but go in the opposite direction, so you get a curly "S" shape.**

   After you get the scrolls started, use your flat-nose pliers to keep the scrolls flat as you work them around.

I like to work both ends toward the middle. That way, both ends end up being the same size. Check out Figure 7-5b. Figure 7-5c shows you the finished "S" scroll. Practice with several pieces, don't be worried how silly the scrolls look at the beginning, you'll get better.

Figure 7-5:
Stages of
the "S"
scroll.

a   b   c

After you're comfortable with this technique, place beads on the wire before you coil the ends up. Check out Project 7-2 to see how to incorporate them into jewelry designs. You can make larger or smaller scrolls, depending on your preference and their role in your design.

Project 7-2: Beaded "S" Scroll Bracelet

Customize the colors in this bracelet to make it your own. I use both gold and silver wire in my design. And I chose bead colors that matched my daughter's birthstone (peridot) and my birthstone (sapphire). Check out Figure 7-7 for a look at the finished project.

Tools and Materials

Round-nose pliers

Flat-nose pliers

7 6-inch pieces of 20-gauge wire, half-hard (I used 4 gold, 3 silver)

7 6mm faceted round glass beads (I used 3 turquoise, 4 peridot)

8 jump rings, silver

1 lobster claw clasp, silver

1. **Place 1 glass bead on each piece of wire.**

2. **Twist each piece into an "S" scroll as shown in Figures 7-5a and b.**
   Take a look at Figure 7-6a to see a finished scroll.

Figure 7-6:
Steps to
complete
the beaded
scroll
bracelet.

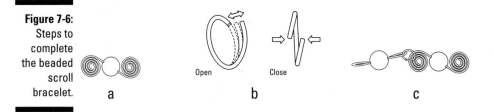

a   b   c

Open   Close

3. **Repeat Steps 1 and 2 with the remaining 6 wires.**

4. **Open 1 jump ring, like the one in Figure 7-6b.** (Remember, never pull a jump ring open and distort the round shape. Just bend it sideways to open it.)

5. **Connect 2 scrolls together by place one end of a scroll in the jump ring. Place one end of a second scroll in the same jump ring. Gently squeeze the jump ring to return it to its original shape.** See Figure 7-6c. Repeat this process until all the scrolls are connected in a single chain.

6. **Use the lobster clasp to join each end of the chain to form the bracelet. Use jump rings to connect the clasp to the scrolls.**

First, try your hand at tight coils, as shown in the following steps. You don't need pliers to do this, but it's good practice.

1. **Cut about 6 inches of wire and insert the end into the jaws of flat-nose pliers, holding with one hand.** With the other hand, hold a pencil or pen.

2. **Holding the wire and pen together, wrap the wire around the pen with the other hand, creating a coil, as shown in Figure 7-8a.** Keep working until you've made an even, tight coil, and then remove the pen. Voila! A cute little coil appears! Check out Figure 7-8b for the finished product.

Figure 7-7:
Beaded "S"
Scroll
Bracelet.

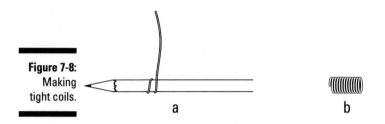

Figure 7-8:
Making
tight coils.

You can find tools that can help you twist coils in no time. They can even help you make coils from your coils! Look for brand names like Twist 'n' Curl or Wire Worker coiling tool available at most crafts stores.

Now, give loop de loops a try. Using your round-nose pliers, simply wrap your wire around once to create a small loop about ¼-inch wide. Look at Figure 7-9a for an example. Repeat the loop several times. Keep repeating until you've made several even loops, as in Figure 7-9b. It's not as easy as it looks, but keep working at it.

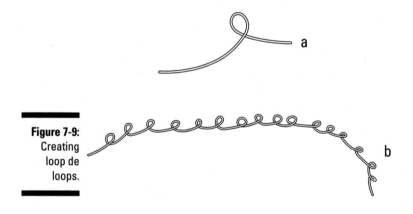

Figure 7-9:
Creating
loop de
loops.

Creating an eye loop

One of the most basic, but often used, wire-working techniques is the eye loop. An *eye loop* basically adds a loop to a piece of wire to make it connectable. This technique is often used to connect beads together and add dangles to earrings, bracelets, or necklaces. Check out Figure 7-10 for examples of how the finished loop looks.

The following steps show you how to use eye loops to make a dangle for an earring, a necklace, or a charm bracelet.

1. **Take a 2-inch headpin and add a bead to it.**

2. **Then take your flat-nose pliers and bend the wire to create a 90-degree angle, like the one in Figure 7-10a.**

3. **Trim your headpin so that only ½-inch of wire remains.**

4. **Use your round-nose pliers to bend the end of the wire back to begin to create the eye, as in Figure 7-10b. Reposition your pliers, if necessary, to complete the loop.** Check out Figure 7-10c for the finished eye.

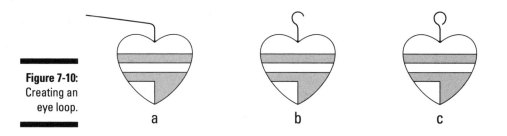

Figure 7-10: Creating an eye loop.

a b c

Now add your dangles to a pair of earwires or hooks, you have an easy pair of earrings to keep for yourself or to give as a nice gift. Check out the "Attaching pieces together" section later in this chapter for details on connecting your dangles to other pieces. When you're feeling confident about your eye-making techniques, try using silver or gold headpins, and use semiprecious stones to match a special outfit.

Wrapping loops

Creating wrapping loops is a slightly more advanced technique in wire wrapping, but not tough to tackle. Basically, you're creating an eye loop on the end of a head pin or piece of wire and wrapping the wire decoratively around itself to create a professional-looking component. It's a terrific technique that you can quickly master, and then build on to create interesting designs from everything from bracelets, to eyeglass chains, earrings, and more. Just follow these steps:

1. **Cut an 8-inch piece of practice wire.**

2. **Using your round-nose pliers, create a loop in the middle of the wire and end up with a 90-degree angle about ⅓ of the way down the wire.** Take a look at Figure 7-11a for reference.

3. **Hold the loop with your round-nose pliers, and use your fingers to wrap the short end of the wire around the straight piece of wire that is directly under your loop. If the wire is hard, use your flat-nose pliers to**

hold the loose wire and wrap it around. Check out Figure 7-11b to see how it works.

4. **Continue to wrap the wire as many times as you want, and if necessary, trim off excess wire. Use bent-nose pliers to press the wire-wrapped end flat to make sure it doesn't stick out and scratch or poke the wearer of your jewelry. File the end of the wire if sharp or pointed.**

5. **If necessary, use your round-nose pliers to reshape and straighten the loop.** Take a look at Figure 7-11c for the finished wrapped loop.

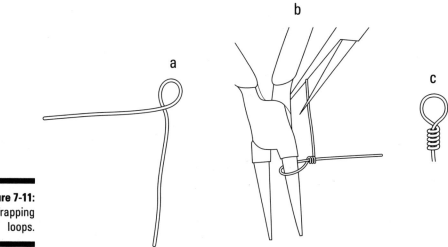

Figure 7-11:
Wrapping
loops.

If you're adding a wrapped loop to both sides of a bead, don't wrap too closely to the bead. Leave a little room when you're first starting out or you could crack the bead.

Add a loop and single wrap to both sides of a bead, and then connect both ends to other components. It stretches out your bead budget, while lengthening your chain.

Creating wrapped beads

When you want to experiment with beads and wire, create wrapped beads, follow these steps:

1. **String a glass bead onto an 8-inch piece of wire.**

2. **Make an eye loop and wrap on one end of the wire like the one in Figure 7-11c.**

3. **Slide your bead onto the opposite end of the wire. Create an eye loop and start to wrap the excess around the wire between the eye and the bead, but don't trim it this time.** Check out Figure 7-12a.

4. **Instead, bring the excess down across the bead and wrap it around the opposite eye loop.** Figures 7-12b and 7-12c shows you how this works.

5. **After you have an adequate wrap, trim the excess. File down any sharp edges.** Figure 7-12d shows you the finished bead wrap.

Figure 7-12:
Wrapping
beads.

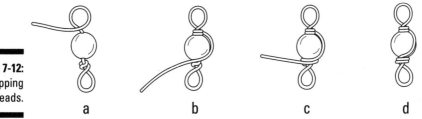

a   b   c   d

This technique is great to create eyeglass cords, rosaries, or even necklaces. Mix wrapped beads with chain for a super fast, trendy design.

Incorporating Wire-Wrapping Techniques in Jewelry Design

All the techniques in this chapter are basic, but when combined, they help you create a wide range of complicated or simple and elegant jewelry. Try Project 7-3 to combine several techniques into a simple, but beautiful design. Finish off a basic bead with a wrapping loop on each end, and then make more to create a chain.

Project 7-3: Wrapped Beaded Earrings

This project combines many of the skills we develop in this chapter, like making "S" scrolls, creating wrapping loops, and creating wrapped beads. I used semi-precious stones, poppy jasper and carnelian, but any round beads you have would work, especially when you're practicing. Take a look at Figure 7-14 for the finished project.

Tools and Materials

Round-nose pliers

Wire cutters

Flat-nose pliers

Jeweler's file

Approximately 16 inches of 22-gauge,
half-hard round sterling wire

2 6mm round poppy jasper beads

2 8mm round carnelian beads

2 2-inch eye pins, sterling silver

2 lever back earwires, sterling silver

1. **Thread one poppy jasper bead onto an eye pin. Follow it with one earwire.** Make a wrapped loop (refer to Figure 7-11c) on the open end of the pin. Make sure the loop of the earwire ends up inside the new wrapped loop before you close it up. Set this aside.

2. **Use your wire cutters to cut the 22-gauge wire into 2 equal parts (each approximately 8 inches in length). Using approximate 3 inches of one piece of wire, create half of an "S" scroll on one end the wire.** Check out Figure 7-13a.

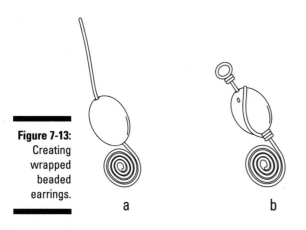

Figure 7-13:
Creating
wrapped
beaded
earrings.

a   b

3. **Thread one carnelian bead onto the straight end of the wire. Use the wrapped bead technique to make one loop. Finish the wrap between the scroll and the bead.** Take a look at Figure 7-13b.

4. **Connect the two components by opening the eye on the jasper component and sliding on the eye loop of the carnelian wrap. Gently close and reshape the eye of the eyepin.**

5. **Repeat the Steps 1 through 4 to create a matching earring.**

Figure 7-14:
Wrapped
Beaded
Earrings.

If you're bead budget doesn't allow you to buy semi-precious stones, substitute similarly colored glass beads.

Gettin' Jiggy with It: Wire Jig Projects

A *jig* is short for a "thing-a-ma-jig," which is a board (made from wood, metal, or plastic) with holes and pegs that fit into those holes. You simply move the pegs to match the pattern you're creating, and then wrap your wire around the pegs. You can create an infinite number of patterns, from simple to very elaborate. Check out Figure 7-15 for a few simple jig patterns.

Jigs are a great way to make lots of wire designs and ensure that they are all uniform in shape and size. The small jigs cost about $10 and the larger intricate ones can be up to $50. If you're handy, you can even make your own jig by nailing some thick nails and screws in an even pattern into a piece of wood.

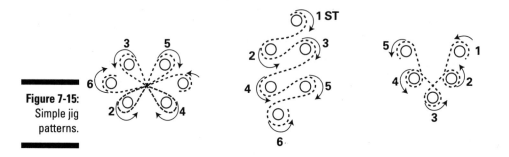

Figure 7-15:
Simple jig
patterns.

If you have a local bead store, you may find some jigs there. Most crafts stores like Michaels, Hobby Lobby, and JoAnn's sell jigs as well. WigJig is a big-name maker of jigs, and is sold through stores or companies like Rio Grande and Fire Mountain Gems. Or check out WigJig's Web site www.wigjig.com to buy a jig or other wire-working tools. They also have a great selection of patterns and wire jewelry projects.

Many jigs come with a booklet of patterns you can follow to make your own custom charms and jewelry components. Choose a transparent plastic jig that lets you place patterns under your jig to make arranging your pegs much easier.

Project 7-4: Celtic Earrings

Celtic designs often employ twists and knots, perfect elements for wire-wrapped jewelry. Use this simple jig pattern in Figure 7-16a to wrap your way to these beautiful earrings. See the completed piece in Figure 7-18.

Tools and Materials

Wire cutter

Wire jig

Jewelers' files

Flat- or bent-nose pliers

Round-nose pliers

2 pieces 20-gauge wire, half hard wire, approximately 10 inches each

2 6mm teardrop beads, top drilled

2 head pins, 2 inches long

2 ear wires

1. **Start by arranging 8 pegs into the shape of a large diamond on your jig.** Check out Figure 7-16a to see what it should look like.

2. **Start with one piece of wire. Insert a small amount of wire into a hole near peg 1. This step helps keep the wire tight as you wrap. Wrap the wire around peg 1 in a clockwise direction.** Figure 7-16b shows you how.

3. **Continue by wrapping the wire around the 3 sets of middle pegs so you create 3 figure-eights. For the top pegs, work clockwise. For the bottom pegs, work counterclockwise.** Figure 7-16c and 7-16d marks your progress.

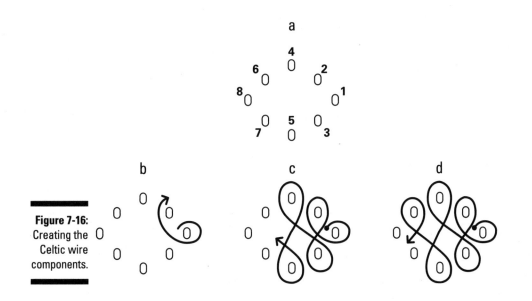

Figure 7-16:
Creating the
Celtic wire
components.

4. **Finish the wire component by wrapping the wire around peg number 8 in a clockwise direction.**

5. **Remove the wire component from your jig, and trim off the excess wire at either the beginning or the end of the component if necessary.** Use jewelers' files to file the rough ends of the piece.

6. **Repeat Steps 2 through 5 with the second wire. Set both wire components aside.** They should resemble Figure 7-17a.

7. **Place a teardrop bead on a head pin.** Create a wrap loop (refer to Figure 7-11c). Your finished teardrop component should look something like Figure 7-17b.

8. **Hang the teardrop component from the end of one of the wire components. Use round-nose pliers to close the loop of the wire component around so the teardrop is secure.** Take a look at Figure 7-17c and Figure 7-18 if you need help.

9. **Add an ear hook to the top of the component (opposite the teardrop) to finish off the project.**

10. **Repeat Steps 7 through 9 with the second teardrop and component.**

Figure 7-17:
Adding
a teardrop
to the
Celtic wire
components.

Figure 7-17:
Adding
a teardrop
to the
Celtic wire
components.

a   b   c

Figure 7-18:
Celtic
Wrapped
Earrings.

Making Your Own Clasps

Jewelry stores, catalogs, and Web sites are full of clasps and other findings in every finish, and style imaginable. But often, I decide to create a simple clasp myself, especially to add to wire-wrapped designs. In this section, I show you how to make two of the most basic clasps.

Hook and eye clasp

The hook and eye clasp is about as basic as they come. It's a figure-eight that connects to a simple, but elegant hook. Look at Figure 7-19d for a look at the finished clasp. This clasp is particularly good for necklaces, because the weight of the necklace usually keeps the necklace flat to the skin. If the clasp doesn't stay flat, as in a bracelet, it can come unhooked and you could lose your piece.

Tools and Materials

Wire cutters	*Round-nose pliers*
Jeweler files	*Flat-nose pliers*
Ruler	*3½ inches of 18-gauge round wire, full hard*

1. **Cut a 2-inch piece of wire.** File both ends smooth.

2. **Using your round-nose pliers, make the smallest possible curl on one end of the wire** (refer to Figure 7-5a).

3. **Use your round-nose pliers and make a larger loop on the opposite end of the wire, curling toward the little loop.** Check out Figure 7-19a to see how it looks. Your large loop will connect to your jewelry, while the little loop will be the decorative end of the hook.

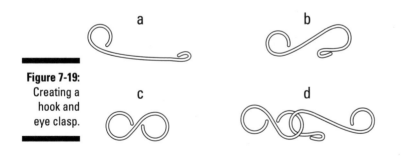

Figure 7-19:
Creating a
hook and
eye clasp.

4. **Use your round-nose pliers to create the hook. Hold your wire perpendicular to your work surface with the large loop at the bottom and the small loop at the top, with the loops facing away from you. Position your pliers just under the small loop.** Bend the wire away toward you so that it forms a hook, like the one in Figure 17-19b. Set your hook aside.

5. **File the ends of the remaining 1½ inches of wire.**

6. **Use your round-nose pliers to make a loop like the one in Step 3. Repeat it on the other end, in the opposite direction.** Create a figure-eight like the one in Figure 7-19c. Figure 7-19d shows you the finished clasp.

"S" hook clasp

The "S" hook is a simple and elegant way to finish a bracelet or necklace. Check out Figure 7-20c for the finished clasp. Use a heavy gauge wire, because each time you open and close this clasp, you actually bend the clasp. If you're using gold, use 10kt or 14kt because anything higher will be too soft and will create a weak clasp.

Tools and Materials

Wire cutters

Jeweler's files

3 inches each 18-gauge wire, sterling silver

1. **File the ends of your wire pieces smooth.**

2. **Make a small loop at each end of the wire with the tip your round-nose pliers.** One loop should face up and the other down. Check out Figure 7-20a.

3. **Use the wider part of round-nose pliers to create the larger curves in the "S" clasp. Hold the wire with a loop facing away from you.** Position your pliers about ¾ inch from the loop. Gently, bend the wire toward you to create a large loop. Yours should look like Figure 7-20b.

4. **Repeat Step 3 with the other end of the wire to create an "S" like the one in Figure 7-20 c.**

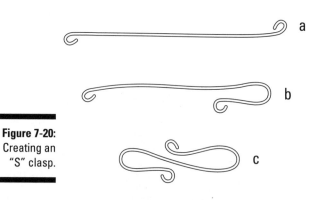

Figure 7-20:
Creating an
"S" clasp.

5. **Connect this clasp to your piece with jump rings, or create and eye clasp using the instructions in the "Hook and eye clasp" section.** Then gently bend one side of the "S" clasp and insert it through the eye for your finished clasp.

For an added touch of elegance, add a delicate dangle to the stationary part of the "S."

Project 7-5: "S" Wire Earrings

To get a little extra practice creating "S" hooks, try these easy, fun earrings. Add beads before you bend them to dress them up a bit. Join several together to add glamour. Check out Figure 7-21 for the finished project.

Tools and Materials

Round-nose pliers

Wire cutters

Jeweler's files

2 pieces, 3 inches each 18-gauge wire, sterling silver

2 ear wires, sterling silver

1. **Create an "S" clasp like the one in Figure 7-20c, but before bending the last loop, slide an earwire onto the straight end.** Complete the "S."

2. **Repeat Step 1 with the second piece of wire.**

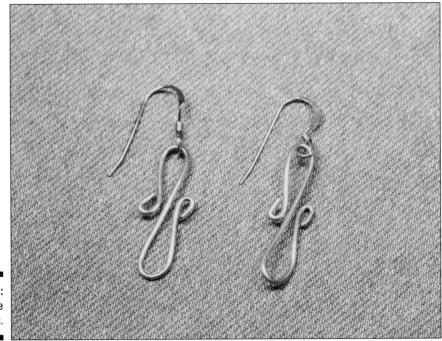

Figure 7-21:
"S" Wire
Earrings.

Part III

Implementing Design Ideas, Trends, and More

"Well, let's see. I have a silver kitty and some bugle beads, but I'm fresh out of skulls and iron crosses."

In this part . . .

I give you projects — lots and lots of projects. Most come with complete step-by-step instructions, illustrations, and photos to show you how to create beautiful jewelry on your own. And look for tips on changing the designs to make them your own.

Each chapter in this part has a separate theme. As with any For Dummies book, you can work on them in any order you prefer. Watch for chapters on making trendy, everyday designs (Chapter 8) or creating the perfect piece for a special occasion (Chapter 9). And Chapter 10 is a must-read chapter if you're interested in creating inspired ethnic designs.

Chapter 8

Creating Fun, Funky Jewelry for Everyday Wear

*B*y their very nature, design trends are always changing. Stay on top of them by watching what people are wearing. Watch celebrity-watcher shows like *Entertainment Tonight, Extra!*, or anything on the E! network. Read "chick" magazines, like *InStyle, Glamour, Cosmopolitan, People, US Weekly*, and anything else that shows photos of what the celebs are wearing.

Awards shows, like the Oscars, Video Music Awards, Golden Globes, and so on, are a great chance to see what stars think is going on in jewelry designs. Actually, the Internet the day after the shows air is even a better way to check out the trends. Look at portal Web sites like www.yahoo.com, www.msn.com, or www.aol.com (if you're a member). These sites almost always have a big link to check out a slideshow of the stars on the red carpet.

I keep a little sketchpad with me when I'm researching jewelry trends or just looking at magazines. Drawing the design (or the elements of the design that catch my fancy) helps me remember the design and start working it over in my mind.

In this chapter, I cover everyday jewelry based on hot trends in several categories: earrings, necklaces, and bracelets. I also give you some projects for other everyday items that don't fit neatly into those categories.

Earring Essentials

Earrings are often the very first jewelry-making projects that people decide to tackle. It's easy and inexpensive to get started, because you just need a couple of tools (round-nose pliers and a wire cutters) and a few supplies (beads and earring findings). Basically, if you can bend a paperclip, you can make an earring. In this section, I give ideas on what's hot now and how to incorporate your ideas into them. Plus, I give you a couple of fun earring projects you can make in minutes.

This section isn't the only place to look for great earring projects. You can find them in just about every chapter of the book, so definitely flip through the book and grab your pliers!

Identifying the hottest earring trends

Any Web search for "trendy earrings" or the like provides you with thousands of design options. I totally recommend that you perform Web searches for different styles of earrings on different Web search engines. I do this regularly and hardly ever find the same thing twice. I get inspired every time I sit down to research.

Here's a list of current earring design trends:

✔ **Shoulder dusters** are long, flowing earrings that almost touch the wearer's shoulders, hence the name. They are usually made up of several (4 to 5 or more) dangles each 4 or more inches long. Make your own by using pre-made chain to create long dangles and connect small beaded headpins to them.

✔ **Chandelier earrings** have been a hot trend in jewelry fashion for several years. Chandeliers employ hoops, triangles, teardrops and other shaped frames that have several holes, each to hold a flowing dangle. You can buy findings or create your own by wrapping wire into loops and hanging them from an earwire. Check out Projects 9-8 and 10-4 (in Chapters 9 and 10, respectively) to see how to make the fashion hotties yourself.

- **Hoops** have been around as long as people have been piercing their bodies. The earliest earrings may have been hoops, because they didn't require any fancy findings or connectors. Hoops continue to gain popularity. (After I saw Olivia Newton-John at the end of *Grease,* I know I was hooped, er, I mean, hooked.) Look for hoops to bead, hoops to hang beads from, hoops to wrap beads onto, and hoops to wear all by themselves.

- **Dangles** hang down from the ear. An earring can be made up of several dangles (as in the case of shoulder duster and chandeliers), or it can have a single lone dangle of any size. Even hoop earrings can have dangles. They are an often-used design component and very simple to make.

- **Posts** are the not-so-fancy earrings that were your starter set. (In fact, if someone has more than one set of ear piercing, chances are post earrings are worn daily in one of them.) But posts have come along way since they made an appearance in the piercing gun. Many people prefer posts because they offer the security of an *earnut,* the little component that slides or screws onto the post, holding it behind your ear. Many *earstud* findings have loops to add dangles or chandeliers. Some have precious gems, semi-precious stones, and crystals set into them for a unique design appeal.

Look for earstuds with posts or cups attached. You can glue half-drilled beads on them to make your own simple studs. Beautiful!

Not every set of earrings fits into these nice, neat categories. You could have a dangle earring that's mounted on a post earring finding. Or chandelier earrings that are so long that they're considered shoulder dusters. Don't let these categories limit you. Merging or morphing existing trends often starts the next trend.

Pausing for practicality

The number-one practical consideration in earring design is metal sensitivity. Many people can't tolerate cheap, base metal earwires and posts. Most people can tolerate components made from surgical steel, which was developed for use in surgical instruments. It has a very low intolerance rate. Even precious metal isn't always tolerated by everyone. Depending on the purity of the metal, the other metals used in the alloys, some people may have trouble tolerating it. For information on metals, alloys, and how they connect with jewelry making, check out Chapter 2.

If you're going to offer your jewelry for sale, your best bet is to use precious metals or surgical steel components for the actual posts or wires. The price will be a bit more expensive, but sensitive customers will thank you.

Another important part of earring design is holding the earring in the wearer's ear. For particularly heavy earrings, consider using posts with *clutches*. A clutch is stronger than an earnut, but performs the same function: It holds heavier earrings in the ear. They may be made of rubber or metal and rubber. Some even have a plastic disk attached to help distribute the weight of the earring across the earlobe rather than just at the piercing hole.

If you love wearing earwires like I do, consider using safety nuts or rubber earnuts. They are small plastic or rubber disks that slide up the wire and keep your beautiful dangles in your ear. They don't support the weight of an earring, but they will provide an extra measure of safety.

Don't neglect your potential non-pierced customers. Gone are the days of the one-size-fits-all "grandma clips"! You can find clip-on earring findings in many styles and metals, including hinge-back clips that look like leaverbacks and screw-findings that allow you to hang dangles from them.

Project 8-1: Venetian Glass Drop Earrings

The great thing about Venetian glass is that it's made by hand, so even within the same set of beads, you find variation. I can spend all day looking at these beauties noticing subtle differences among them. I fell in love with these drop beads at a tiny bead shop in Tucson, Arizona, on a recent vacation. You probably won't find their twins, but find a pair you love and make these easy, beautiful earrings. You can see them in Figure 8-1.

Tools and Materials

Wire cutters

Round-nose pliers

2 25mm Venetian glass teardrop beads, light green with gold swirls

2 6mm smoky topaz bicone crystals

2 2-inch jeweled headpins, sterling silver

2 leaverback earring findings, sterling silver

1. **Slide one glass teardrop onto a headpin. Top it with a crystal.**

2. **Using your wire cutters, trim the end of the headpin, if necessary, to leave about ½ inch of wire above the crystal. Begin to make an eye loop, but before closing the loop, slide on the loop for one leaverback. Close the loop.**

3. **Repeat Steps 1 and 2 to create a second earring.**

Figure 8-1:
Venetian
Glass Drop
Earrings.

Project 8-2: Big and Small Bauble Earrings

Bauble is a fancy word that means cheap-looking or showy trinkets. When the trinkets in this set are combined the effect is hardly cheap. Instead it's fun and playful. I *articulated* several pieces, or gave them independent motion, rather than stringing all the beads together on a single headpin. This technique gives each section some independent movement that helps them catch the light and sparkle. Take a look at these beauties in Figure 8-2.

Tools and Materials

Wire cutters

Round-nose pliers

2 1-inch headpins, gold

6¾-inch eyepins, gold

2 ear hooks, gold

2 5mm bicone crystals, AB finish

2 12mm oval lampwork beads, Aqua with some bumps and swirls

2 6mm faceted round crystals, AB finish

2 7mm faceted round crystals, Aqua

2 5mm round jade beads

1. **Slide one bicone crystal on a headpin. Follow it with 1 lampwork bead.** Begin to make an eye loop at the top of the headpin, but before closing the loop, slide on the loop of one eyepin. Close the loop. See Chapter 7 for help making eye loops.

2. **Slide a 6mm AB crystal on the open end of the eyepin. Begin to make an eye loop above the crystal, but before closing the loop, slide on the loop of another eyepin. Close the loop.**

3. **Slip an aqua crystal on the open end of the eyepin. Begin to make an eye loop above the crystal, but before closing the loop, slide on the loop of another eyepin. Close the loop.**

4. **Thread a jade bead on this eyepin. Begin to make an eye loop above the jade bead, but before closing the loop, slide on the loop of one ear hook. Close the loop.**

5. **Repeat Steps 1 through 4 to complete the second earring.**

These earrings look great with the Glass Bead Necklace with Pendant in Project 8-4. Just use coordinating bead colors, and you'll have a complete set.

Figure 8-2:
Beautiful
Bauble
Earrings.

Nifty Necklaces

Necklaces have never been hotter. Designers borrow from every era, culture, and age to bring us a variety of necklace styling. Whether you're stringing a simple pendant on a cord or weaving an intricate pattern in a beaded collar, there's no shortage of inspiration. In this section, I show you what's hot now and give you hints on following trends in the future. And I also give you several projects to start working your own necklace mojo.

Noticing necklace nuances

Just about every jewelry-making technique is appropriate for making necklaces. (I can't think of a single one that's not good for necklaces, but I'm sure if I make such a bold, definite statement, someone will write me to let me know that I'm wrong.) Whether it's weaving, looming, stringing, knotting, wire-wrapping, it has a place in creating necklaces. The variety in design comes in when you mix techniques, vary the lengths, change components, and mix them all together. Check out Table 8-1 for the names for the various necklace lengths.

Table 8-1	Approximate Necklace lengths	
Name	*Length (in Inches)*	*Description and Suggestions*
Collar	12–13	Made up of multiple strands, worn tight on the neck
Choker	14–16	Usually a single strand, worn right above the collar bone
Princess	17–19	Falls below the collar bone; great with pendants
Matinee	20–24	Falls on the breastbone; great with tassels and dangles
Opera length	28–34	Very dramatic; can be double looped around the neck
Rope	35+	Can be triple looped or worn as multi-loop bracelet

Here are some of the hottest trends in necklaces today:

- ✔ **Y-necklaces** are cool necklaces that have a single dangle in the middle. Look at Project 8-5 in this chapter and Project 9-1 in Chapter 9 for instruction to create your own Y-necklace.

- ✔ **Illusion necklaces** have beads that appear to float on the wearer. They're made with clear thread or cord and beads are glued, knotted, or crimped into place along the length of the strand. Project 2-1 in Chapter 2 gives you all the information you need to create your own.

- ✔ **Lariats** are made from a single long strand of beads that can be wrapped, twisted, and tied in a variety of different designs. The traditional lariat design folds a 36+-inch strand of beads in half, creating a loose loop. The wearer drapes the loop and the ends around to the chest; the ends are tucked through the loop to hold the piece together.

- ✔ **Chokers** have never been hotter. Whether it's a simple memory wire design, an exquisite pendant threaded on silk ribbon, or classic pearls, chokers continue to be hot.

Necklace necessities

With necklaces, it's important to balance comfort and fashion. Anytime you're using wire-wrapping techniques or cutting wire, make sure to sand the cut edges to keep from poking the wearer.

When designing tight fitting necklaces (like collars, chokers, or even princess length) for plus-size women, add 2 to 3 inches to the design. They will enjoy the same look, even though technically the change in length may move them into another category of necklace. Check out the Cheat Sheet (yellow tear out sheet at the beginning of this book) for my specific recommendations.

Project 8-3: Front Toggle Necklace

This necklace shows off the beauty of the hottest trend in jewelry clasps at the moment, the toggle clasp. It measures approximately 35 inches, plus 2 extra inches of dangle.

Tools and Materials

Wire cutters

Round-nose pliers

Flat-nose pliers

Ruler

1 toggle clasp, gold-tone

36-inch chain, gold-tone

2¾-inch headpins, gold

8 1-inch eyepins, gold

6 9mm round glass beads, topaz-colored

4 20mm lampwork fish shaped beads, brown

2 split jump rings, gold-tone

1. **Using your wire cutters, cut a 2-inch piece of chain. Set aside.**

2. **Slide one round bead onto a head pin. Begin to create an eye loop, but before closing the loop, slip the end of one piece of chain onto the wire. Close the eye loop. Set aside.** Chapter 7 can help you make an eye loop.

3. **Repeat Steps 1 and 2 to create a second bead and chain dangle.**

4. **Open one jump ring. (Take a look at Chapter 7 if you need help.) Slide both chain dangles onto the jump ring. Add the loop from the T end of the toggle clasp. Attach the remaining long piece of chain. Close your jump ring.** Your piece should look like Figure 8-3a. Set aside.

5. **Slip one of the remaining round beads onto a headpin, begin to make an eye loop, but leave it slightly open.** (You'll connect to the chain in a few minutes.) Set aside.

6. **Repeat Step 6 with all the remaining round sand fish beads.** Your beads should look like Figure 8-3b.

7. **Measure approximately 3 to 4 inches up the chain from your jump ring. Cut the chain. Set the long piece aside. Connect the eyepin from one of your fish beads in Step 6 to the remaining chain. Attach the other end of the eye pin to the long piece of chain.**

8. **Repeat Step 7, alternating round and fish beads and leaving 3 to 4 inches of chain between bead elements.** Figure 8-3c shows a section of chain with round and fish bead elements. Continue until all your beads and chain are used.

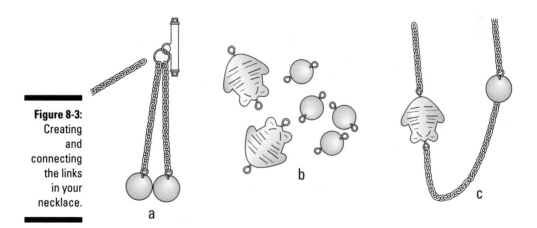

Figure 8-3:
Creating
and
connecting
the links
in your
necklace.

9. **Open your last jump ring. Slide it onto the end of your chain. Slide the loop from the round end of the toggle clasp onto the jump ring. Gently close the jump ring.** Figure 8-4 shows the finished necklace.

10. **Slip the finished necklace around your neck and wear the toggle in the front.**

Figure 8-4:
Front Toggle
Necklace.

Project 8-4: Glass Beaded Necklace with Pendant

This necklace makes me want to go on vacation. The calming blues and greens make me feel like I have a boat drink in my hand. Check out the completed project in Figure 8-5.

Tools and Materials

Wire cutters

Crimp pliers

Flat-nose pliers

Bead board (optional)

35mm teardrop glass pendant with bail (the loop a pendant hangs by) in aqua, blue, and yellow

42 seed beads size 8/0, aqua

30 seed beads size 8/0, blue

12 seed beads size 8/0, clear

6 3mm round glass beads, clear

6 18mm oval lampwork beads, aqua with green and white swirls

6 7mm faceted round crystal, aqua

6 10mm, light green glass beads (I used two of three different styles, one style was a straight rectangle, the other was slightly rounded rectangle, and the third was oval)

24 inches nylon coated stainless steel beading wire, 0.10–0.15-inch diameter

2 2x2mm crimp beads, silver

1 fancy toggle clasp, silver

1. **Thread one crimp bead onto the wire. Follow it with the loop from one piece of the toggle clasp. Rethread the wire through the crimp bead. Pull the wire to create a small loop wire around the loop on the clasp. Gently crimp the bead with your crimp pliers. Trim away the excess wire with your wire cutters.** For a visual example, take a look at Chapter 2.

Adding the end of the clasp now keeps you for having to wrestle the strand from both ends as you're stringing. It's one less thing to worry about, so get it done early.

2. **Begin stringing the beads. String your beads in this order: 3 blue seed beads, 3 aqua seed beads, 3 blue seed beads, 3 aqua seed beads. Follow with one 10mm light green oval bead. Next is 1 3mm clear bead, followed by 3 blue seed beads, 3 aqua seed beads, and 1 7mm faceted aqua bead. Follow with 1 3mm clear bead, followed by 3 blue seed beads, 3 aqua seed beads, and 3 blue seed beads.**

As you string your beads, slide the beads over the tail of your trimmed wire from Step 1. This covers the tail for a neat and tidy look.

3. **Slide on one lampwork bead. Follow it with 3 clear seed beads, 1 7mm aqua faceted round, 3 aqua seed beads, and one 10mm light green rounded rectangle glass bead, and then 3 blue seed beads.**

4. **Repeat Step 3, but use one straight rectangle 10mm bead instead of the rounded rectangle.**

5. **Slide another lampwork bead onto your strand. Follow it with 3 aqua seed beads, 1 3mm clear bead, and another 3 blue seed beads.**

This point is the center of your necklace. In the next steps, you'll duplicate this pattern on the other side. Because you're working from the middle out (rather than from the outer end toward the middle), you string the beads in the reverse order that you did in Steps 2 through 5.

6. **Slide on your pendant onto the strand. String on 3 blue seed bead, 1 3mm clear bead, followed by 3 aqua seed beads. Add a lampwork bead.**

7. **Holding both ends of your beading wire, fold your necklace in half, with the pendant as the center point. You should see the symmetrical pattern emerging. Continue matching your design up the strand until you reach the end.**

Some people prefer to lay all their beads out on a bead board before they string bead 1. Definitely use that method if it's easier for you. Depending on my mood, I use both methods. I *always* use a bead board when I'm designing a piece; I *sometimes* use one when I'm duplicating a design I've already created. It's strictly personal preference: There's no right or wrong way.

8. **Slide on one crimp bead. Follow it with the loop from the other end of the clasp. Rethread the wire down through the crimp bead, making a loop around the loop of the clasp. Using your crimp pliers, gently hold the crimp bead in place, but don't crimp it. With your other hand, use your flat-nose pliers to pull the wire taut and take up any slack. Gently crimp the bead. Tuck the wire into the hole of the bead next to it. Trim the wire under the bead for a professional finish.** Check out Chapter 9 to see how this works.

Figure 8-5:
Glass
Beaded
Necklace
with
Pendant.

Project 8-5: Fanciful Fairy Y-Necklace

The ever-popular "Y" necklace takes on a mythical feel with this beautiful fairy charm dangle. Use the charm of your choice or large teardrop bead in its place as you like. Take a look at it in Figure 8-6.

Tools and Materials

Round-nose pliers

Wire cutters

Ruler

Flat-nose pliers

Approximately 14 inches of chain, goldtone

5 1½-inch eyepins, goldtone

10 4mm crystal beads, dark amethyst

5 6mm round amethyst beads

1 20mm pewter cast fairy charm, antique goldtone

1 springring clasp, goldtone

3 split jump rings, goldtone

1. **Slide the following beads on an eyepin: crystal, amethyst, crystal. Begin to create an eye loop, but don't close the loop completely.** (You'll use these loops to connect to the chain later on.) Set aside.

2. **Repeat Step 1 with the remaining beads and eyepins for a total of 5 beaded eyepins.** Set aside.

3. **Using your wire cutters, cut a 4 inch piece of chain. Attach one beaded eyepin component to one end of the chain. Close the loop.**

4. **Repeat Step 3.** Set aside.

5. **Using your wire cutters, cut a 2-inch piece of chain. Connect one end of the chain to an eyepin from Steps 3 and 4. Gently open the eyepin, attach the chain, and then close the loop. Connect another beaded eyepin component to the free end of the 2-inch chain. Close the loop.**

6. **Repeat Step 5.** Set aside. You should now have two identical strands assembled from chain sections and eyepin components.

7. **Cut a 1-inch piece of chain. Use it to connect to both of the last two unconnected eyepins on each of your strands. You will now have a single strand made from 4 beaded eyepin components and 5 chain sections.** Set aside.

8. **Create the center "Y" dangle. Cut a 1-inch piece of chain. Connect it to your remaining beaded eyepin component. Close the loop. Attach the other end of the eye pin to your charm.** Set aside.

9. **Open a jump ring. Connect it to one open end of the chain of the "Y" dangle you created in Step 8. Fold in half the strand you created in Steps 1 through 7 so that you can find the middle. Attach the jump ring to the chain at the middle point. Gently close the jump ring.** If you need help opening and closing jump rings, check out Chapter 7.

10. **Open another jump ring. Connect it to one open end of the long chain you created in Steps 1 through 7. Before closing it, slide the loop from the springring clasp onto the jump ring. Close the jump ring.**

11. **Open the last jump ring. Connect it to the last remaining end of chain. This jump ring serves as part of the clasp. Fasten the necklace by connecting your springring to the jump ring.**

Figure 8-6:
Fanciful
Fairy
Y-Necklace.

Brilliant Bracelets

I love bracelets because you can mix and match them. You get the chance to wear multiple designs at the same time. This versatility is especially important after you've created so many terrific designs that it's hard to choose. In this section, I show you how to make several bracelet designs using a variety of techniques and materials.

Identifying design trends

When I first started designing jewelry, only a few bracelet clasp options were available to everyone; the barrel clasp and the spring ring clasp topped the list. While both clasps have their place, it's so exciting that bracelet designs are branching out to include all sorts of clasps, many of which had once been reserved for "fine" jewelry. Designers are incorporating detailed toggle clasps, fancy filigree fishhook clasps, and triple strand box clasps into their designs.

The stretch bracelet is an extremely popular trend that will probably move into the "classic" jewelry design strata at some point. It's made using elastic thread or cord, a continuous strand of beads, without a clasp. Instead the elastic is knotted and usually glued. The wearer then stretches the bracelet to get it on, wearing it snuggly on the wrist. Check out Project 8-6 to make your own.

Employing practical considerations

When making gift jewelry, take special consideration for length, because not everyone wears the same size. For this reason, memory wire and stretch bracelets are good choices if you're not sure of what size someone wears.

Project 8-6: Carnelian and Pearl Stretch Bracelet

You can literally make this bracelet in a matter of minutes. The simple alternating pattern provides for seamless simplicity and elegance. It measures approximately 7 inches in circumference. See Figure 8-7 for a peek at the finished product.

You want a snug fit, but don't want the elastic to show. If this length is too snug, feel free to make this bracelet longer. Each set of beads (one carnelian, one pearl) is about ¼ inch. Just add a few more repetitions to increase it to the right length.

Tools and Materials

Scissors

Binder clip (yep, the ones from an office supply store)

10 inches of 0.05 elastic beading cord, clear

17 6mm carnelian round beads

17 4mm button-shaped freshwater pearls

Hypo-cement, or glue of your choice

1. **Clip your binder clip to one end of your elastic, so that your beads don't slip off as you string them onto the elastic.**

2. **String your beads alternating between carnelian and pearl. Begin with whichever one you want, alternating as you go.**

3. **Remove your binder clip and tie an overhand knot. Dab glue on your knot. Trim away the excess elastic.**

    Don't trim too close to the knot, or it will unravel.

4. **Tuck your newly glued knot inside your last carnelian bead. I recommend using the carnelian to hide the knot because it's bigger. It's just a bit easier.** Allow the glue to dry for 24 hours before wearing the bracelet.

Figure 8-7:
Carnelian
and Pearl
Stretch
Bracelet.

Figure 8-8 shows you a more masculine version of the same bracelet designed by Anthony Dyess, age 12. He used a slightly more complicated pattern (one gold bead, one round hematite bead, one hexagonal hematite tube) and the effect is very trendy. It's a great addition to any jewelry wardrobe.

Figure 8-8:
Hematite
Stretch
Bracelet.

Project 8-7: Garnet and Silver Bracelet

This bracelet is made with only a few materials. Make a lovely and simple design by repeating a simple pattern. This bracelet measures approximately 8 inches; see the finished product in Figure 8-10.

Tools and Materials

Wire cutters

Crimp pliers

Flat-nose pliers

11 3mm round beads, silver

20 7mm garnet faceted teardrop crystals, drilled top to bottom

10 8mm daisy spacer beads, silver

2 2x2mm crimp beads, silver

1 toggle clasp, silver

12 inches nylon coated stainless steel wire

1. **Attach one side of your toggle clasp to your beading wire. Thread one crimp bead onto the wire. Follow it with the loop from one piece of the toggle clasp. Rethread the wire through the crimp bead. Pull the wire to create a small loop wire around the loop on the clasp. Gently crimp the bead with your crimp pliers. With your wire cutters, trim away the excess wire.** To see how this looks, check out the example in Chapter 2.

2. **Begin stringing beads in the following order: round silver bead, garnet (with the small end pointed toward the silver bead), daisy spacer, garnet (the small end pointed away from the daisy spacer).** Check out Figure 8-9 to see how the pattern looks.

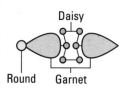

Figure 8-9:
Garnet and silver pattern.

Daisy

Round   Garnet

3. **Repeat the pattern from Step 2 nine more times, for a total of ten on your beading wire. Add one more silver round bead to the end.**

4. **Thread one crimp bead onto the wire. Follow it with the loop from the remaining piece of the toggle clasp. Rethread the wire through the crimp bead. Use your crimp pliers to hold the crimp bead, but don't close it. With your flat-nose pliers in your other hand, pull the wire to create a small loop wire around the loop on the clasp. Pull the wire taut, taking up any slack. Gently crimp the bead with your crimp pliers. Tuck the wire into the first bead in the strand. Trim the wire under the bead for a clean finish.** Check out Chapter 9 for close-up pictures, if you need help.

Figure 8-10:
Garnet and
Silver
Bracelet.

Any simple pattern can be repeated to create a similar bracelet. Check out
Figure 8-11a for the simple pattern that created the Ice Cool Blue Bracelet in
Figure 8-11b.

Figure 8-11:
Pattern of
and finished
look at the
Ice Cool
Blue
Bracelet.

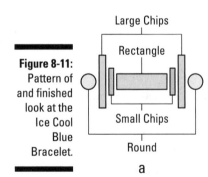

Large Chips

Rectangle

Small Chips

Round

a

b

Project 8-8: Memory Wire Cuff

Memory wire is an extremely versatile product, and you use it as the frame for this bracelet. It's a great project to practice your wire wrapping. Figure 8-13 shows you the finished project.

Tools and Materials

Round-nose pliers

Flat-nose pliers

Wire cutters

1 loop of bracelet size memory wire

1 small spool 26-gauge magenta-colored wire

15 6mm round hematite beads

1. **Using your round-nose pliers, make a loop on one end of the memory wire.** This loop will be your anchor.

2. **Lay a small amount of colored wire flat against the memory wire close to the loop. Wrap the colored wire around itself to help secure it against the memory wire.**

   Work with the colored wire while it's on the spool. It's much easier to handle and will be less likely to get bent or nicked.

3. **Slip a bead onto the memory wire, and then wrap the colored wire over the bead.** Check out Figure 8-12a to see this in action.

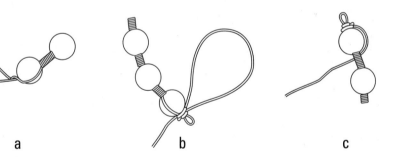

Figure 8-12: Wrapping wire around beads and memory wire.

a   b   c

4. **Wrap colored wire again around the memory wire, approximately four more times.**

   The colored wire is acting like a space bead. You're creating space between the large beads with tight coils of wire.

5. **Repeat Steps 3 and 4 until you've made your way all around the memory wire.**

   Consider using nylon jaw pliers, as necessary, to straighten out your colored wire. The nylon coating helps save the colored wire from getting scratched as you work with it.

6. When you have only ½ inch of unwrapped memory wire left, make a few wraps with your colored wire, and then use your round-nose pliers to make another loop on the end of the memory wire.

7. To help secure the colored wire, insert the end of the colored wire down through the last wrap you did around the last bead. See Figure 8-12b.

8. Continue to bring the colored wire back down around the last bead and make more wraps around the memory wire (between the last two beads) so that you are wrapping around the colored wire again. Check out Figure 8-12c to see how this looks.

9. Use wire cutters to trim off excess wire.

10. Use nylon jaw pliers to press the colored wire in spots around the end of the memory wire to help flatten the colored wire and tighten it around the memory wire. Because the wire is so thin, if you press enough, it will not stick out and scratch the wearer. You can use flat-nose pliers to do this also, but be careful because these pliers can scratch the colored wire.

Figure 8-13 shows you the finished bracelet. Consider using different combinations of beads and colored wire.

Figure 8-13:
Memory
Wire Cuff
Bracelet.

I chose to make this into a cuff style bracelet, but obviously, you could make it longer so that it wraps around your wrist or even do this with necklace size memory wire. While the 26-gauge wire worked well and was easy to handle with my fingers, I think a thicker wire could work well and perhaps show up better, such as a 22-gauge. Also, if I make any more of these, I will probably use beads whose color contrasts more to the wire, so this is something to consider when you try this project.

Project 8-9: Three-Strand Mom's Beaded Bracelet

Mom's rings and pendants (those with stones to match your children's birthstones) have been around for a long time. But this project takes that traditional favorite and updates it. Carrie Henry designed this bracelet. She used three strands in her bracelet, one for each of her kids: Elizabeth, Jared, and Josh. Check out her bracelet in Figure 8-14.

Definitely use a bead board for this project. No two strands will have the exact same mix of alphabet beads to round beads in various sizes, but should have the same length, approximately 7½ inches. A bead board can help you make sure you have enough beads to get the length you need.

Tools and Materials

Wire cutters

Crimp pliers

Flat-nose pliers

Bead board

4mm alphabet beads, enough to spell out your kid(s)' name(s)

2 crystals for each strand, in the color of your kid(s)' birthstones

4mm corrugated round beads, goldtone (2 beads for each strand)

4mm round beads, silvertone (see Table 8-1 for approximate amounts)

3mm round beads, goldtone (see Table 8-2 for approximate amounts)

3mm corrugated round beads, goldtone (see Table 8-2 for approximate amounts)

2mm disk beads, goldtone (see Table 8-2 for approximate amounts)

12 inches of nylon coated stainless steel beading wire for each strand, 0.1-inch diameter

2x2mm crimp beads, 2 per strand

1 toggle clasp

1. **Lay out one child's name in beads on your bead board. In between each letter, place a 3mm round bead as a spacer. Before the first letter and after the last letter, place one crystal to represent the child's birthstone. On either end of the sequence, place a 4mm corrugated bead next to each birthstone crystal.** This sequence represents the middle part of your strand.

2. **Repeat Step 1 with each strand in your bracelet. If possible, lay out each strand directly next to the others.** This step helps you as you build a symmetrical design on each strand, while coordinating it with the others.

3. **Build your pattern on each side of the child's name.** Carrie used 4mm silvertone round beads as spacers. So she placed a 4mm round bead on the outside of the 4mm corrugated bead, and then used a basic pattern of 3mm corrugated, 4mm round bead, 3mm corrugated, 4mm round bead. Then for the short names, she continued this pattern for one more repetition. She finished each end of the strand with a similar, smaller pattern of 2mm gold disk, 4mm round bead, 2mm gold disk, 4mm round bead.

You're building the design from the middle out on your bead board, so work with the patterns on both sides of each name at the same time. As long as they match, and coordinate with the other strands, you're doing a great job! Use a beadboard with three or more grooves to lay out each child's name.

4. **After you've determined that your strands are the same length, set them aside.**

5. **Before stringing the beads, you'll attach each length of coated wire to the "T" side of the toggle clasp. To do this, slide one crimp bead on one wire. Slide the loop of the clasp onto the wire. Rethread the wire through the crimp bead. Take your crimp pliers and gently crimp the bead in place.** Repeat until all three (or whatever number you're using) wires are attached to the "T" side of the toggle clasp.

6. **Start stringing each name and supporting cast of beads onto the beading wire, making sure to tuck the end of the wires into the first bead that you string onto your wire. As you finish each one, attach it to the round end of the toggle clasp. Rethread the wire through the crimp bead. Use your crimp pliers to hold the crimp bead, but don't close it. With your flat-nose pliers in your other hand, pull the wire to create a small loop wire around the loop on the clasp. Pull the wire taut, taking up any slack. Gently crimp the bead with your crimp pliers. Tuck the wire into the first bead in the strand. Trim the wire under the bead for a clean finish.** Check out Chapter 9 for close-up pictures if you need help.

Figure 8-14:
Three-
Strand
Mom's
Beaded
Bracelet.

Project 8-10: Beaded Watch with Interchangeable Band

I make several different bands but keep the same watch face. Each band comes equipped with a lobster claw on each end to snap easily on and off the watch face. I have a crystal strand, a southwestern strand, and a funky glass bead strand. I switch them out as my mood (or occasion) changes. Take a look at Figure 8-15 for the finished project.

Tools and Materials

Wire cutters

Crimp pliers

Flat-nose pliers

Bead board (optional)

1 2-loop watch component (This is a watch face with one loop by the 12 and another by the 6.)

2 lobster claw clasps

7 inches of beads per strand

10 inches of nylon coated stainless steel beading wire for each strand

2 2x2mm crimp beads for each strand

1. **Connect one lobster clasp to your beading wire. Slide on one crimp bead. Follow it with the loop from the clasp. Rethread the wire down through the crimp bead, making a loop around the loop of the clasp. Using your crimp pliers, gently crimp the bead in place.**

2. **String your beads in the order you prefer, making sure you tuck the end of the wires into the first bead that you string onto your wire.** Use a bead board to design your strands, if you like. I find it helps me visualize the project better and saves me the re-stringing time.

3. **After you've strung about 7 inches of beads, attach the second lobster claw clasp. Repeat Step 2; except don't crimp the bead immediately. Instead, use your crimp pliers to gently hold the crimp bead in place, but don't crimp it. With your other hand, use your flat-nose pliers to pull the wire taut and take up any slack. Gently crimp the bead. Tuck the wire into the hole of the bead next to it. With your wire cutters, trim the wire under the bead for a professional finish.** Check out Chapter 9 to see how this works.

4. **Clip each lobster claw clasp to one loop of the watch and enjoy your new accessory!**

Figure 8-15:
Beaded
Watch with
Inter-
changeable
Band.

Making Other Fun Stuff

Jewelry ornamentation doesn't have to be only directed to the neck, ears, and wrists. Many other opportunities exist for decoration and adornment. You can even accessorize your accessories (like cellphones, purses, barrettes and other hair accessories, and key chains) with beads. You really can bead just about anything. For best results use durable beads for items that will get knocked around or dropped. Check out Chapter 12 for specific projects designed to make your home beautiful.

Project 8-11: Semi-Precious Stone Anklet

This anklet goes perfectly with either your leopard print bikini or your soccer mom Capri pants. So it's a definite must-make on all counts! You'll find the final project in Figure 8-16.

This anklet is approximately 11 inches long. You may choose to make yours longer or shorter. Each repetition is about an inch long, so adjust your bead needs accordingly.

Tools and Materials

Wire cutters	*1 jump ring, silver*
Crimp pliers	*11 4mm red jasper cube beads*
Flat-nose pliers	*11 5mm rosebud beads, silver*
Lobster claw clasp, silver	*12 5mm black fringe beads (tiny, teardrop-shaped seed beads)*
13 inches nylon coated stainless steel beading wire	*35 tiger's eye heishe beads (small, thin disks), 2–4mm wide*
2 2x2mm crimp beads, silver	

1. **Thread one crimp bead onto the wire. Follow it with the loop from one piece of the lobster claw clasp. Rethread the wire through the crimp bead. Pull the wire to create a small loop wire around the loop on the clasp. Gently crimp the bead with your crimp pliers. Trim away the excess wire with your wire cutters.** For a visual example, take a look at Chapter 2.

2. **Begin stringing your beads in the following order: tiger's eye, fringe, tiger's eye, rosebud, tiger's eye, and jasper.** Repeat this pattern ten more times for a total of 11.

3. **To balance the design, add a tiger's eye, a fringe bead, and another tiger's eye.**

4. **Attach your jump ring to your strand with a crimp bead. Slide on one crimp bead. Follow it with the jump ring. Rethread the wire down through the crimp bead, making a loop around the loop of the clasp. Using your crimp pliers, gently hold the crimp bead in place, but don't crimp it. With your other hand, use your flat-nose pliers to pull the wire taut and take up any slack. Gently crimp the bead. Tuck the wire into the hole of the bead next to it. With your wire cutters, trim the wire under the bead for a professional finish.** Check out Chapter 9 to see how this works.

Figure 8-16:
Semi-
Precious
Stone
Anklet.

Project 8-12: Peruvian Beaded Key Chain

The beads in this key chain are hand painted ceramic beads from Peru. You can use whatever beads you like, but I warn you not to use too delicate a bead if you want to keep your key chain around for a while. Delicate beads don't hold up well in pockets, purses, backpacks, and anywhere else people may stick their keys. Take a look at the project in Figure 8-17.

Tools and Materials

Wire cutters

Flat-nose pliers

Round-nose pliers

3 ceramic Peruvian beads, assorted sizes and shapes

2–6 4mm blue glass beads (use as needed)

3 surgical steel head pins

1 10mm split jump ring

1 key ring finding

1. **Slide a Peru bead onto a headpin. Use your round-nose pliers to make an eye loop on the end.** Take a look at Chapter 7 if you need help with eye loops.

2. **Repeat Step 1 with remaining ceramic beads.**

   Use the 4mm beads at the top or bottom of any beads with large holes to keep the large beads from slipping off. The smaller beads have smaller holes and act as stoppers for the larger beads.

3. **Open your jump ring. Slip all the eye loops attached to all your head-pins onto the jump ring.**

4. **Slip on the loop from your key chain finding. Gently close your jump ring.** Take a look at Chapter 7 for help opening and closing jump rings.

Figure 8-17:
Peruvian
Beaded Key
Chain.

Project 8-13: Hematite Eyeglass Cord

Connect these to your reading glasses or give them as a gift to your favorite hardworking teacher (or writer, hint, hint). Check out the finished project in Figure 8-19.

Tools and Materials

Flat-nose pliers

Round-nose pliers

Scissors

24 inches size 4 nylon thread with attached needle

2 clamshell bead tips, silver

Hypo-cement, or glue of your choice (optional)

12 4mm bicone crystals, AB finish

120 3mm round hematite beads

4 12mm fancy oblong beads, silver

2 6mm star hematite beads

2 split jump rings, silver

1 pair eyeglass holder findings, with corrugated silver balls attached (take a look at Figure 8-18a for a peek at these)

1. **String your thread through one clamshell bead tip. Tie a knot at the end of your thread inside the bead tip. Tie another knot as close to the first as possible. If you like, add a dab of glue to the knots. Trim the end of the thread. With your flat-nose pliers, close the clamshell around the knots.** Check out Figure 8-18b and 8-18c to see this in action.

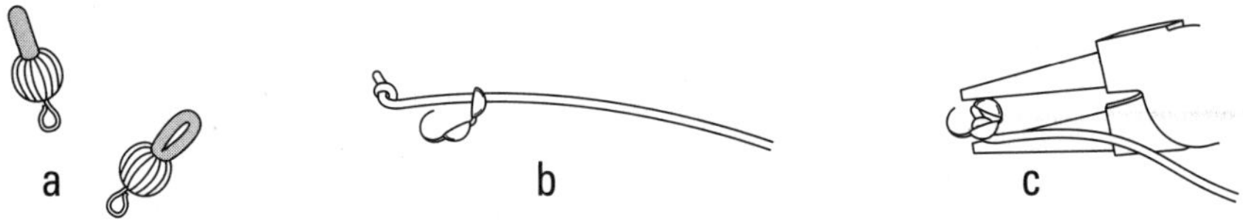

Figure 8-18:
Eyeglass
holder
findings
and steps
to attach
a bead tip.

a   b   c

2. **Begin stinging your beads in the following order: 8 hematite round beads, 1 crystal, one fancy silver bead, 1 crystal, 4 hematite round beads, 1 crystal, 1 hematite star, 1 crystal, 4 hematite round beads, one crystal, 1 fancy silver, 1 crystal.**

3. **Next string 88 hematite round beads. Then repeat the pattern from Step 2 backward: 1 crystal, 1 fancy silver, 1crystal, 4 hematite round beads, 1 crystal, 1 hematite star, 1 crystal, 4 hematite round beads, 1 crystal, 1 fancy silver bead, 1 crystal, 8 hematite round beads.**

4. **String your last clamshell bead tip. Repeat the remainder of Step 1, cutting off the string close to the knot before applying the glue.**

Always string the clamshell so that its "mouth" is pointing away from the beads. You close the clamshell around the knots to secure them.

5. Open a jump ring. Slide on the loop attached to one eyeglass finding.
   Close the jump ring. Repeat with the second jump ring and finding.

6. Use your round-nose pliers to bend the hook of the bead tip around
   the jump ring. Repeat with the second bead tip and jump ring.

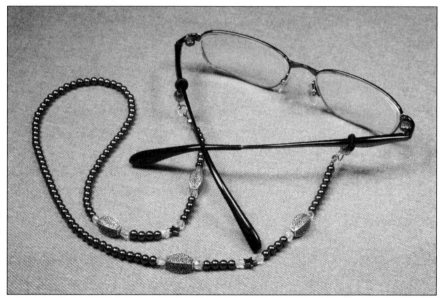

Figure 8-19:
Hematite
Eyeglass
Cord.

Chapter 9

Crafting Your Own Evening, Bridal, and Holiday Jewelry

Custom-designed jewelry is a great addition to any special event. Sometimes it's tough to find that perfect piece to make the statement you're looking for right off the shelf. Or in many cases, you know exactly what you want, but can't afford to pay the retail markup. Many jewelry makers get their start by designing a single piece for a special event.

In this chapter, I show you the basic steps I use when designing special-occasion jewelry. Then I give you specific design tips and projects for a few special occasions, like a night on the town, a bride's big day, and a slew of fun holidays.

Understanding the Basic Design Process

Often, I see a particular bead (or group of beads) that inspires me to create special occasion jewelry. A perfect example is the Patriotic Polymer Clay Necklace in Project 9-11 later in this chapter. I found a set of red, white, and blue polymer beads, and then designed the piece to use them with.

Here are the general steps I follow:

1. **Lay your central beads down on your bead board.** A bead board is an indispensable designing tool. It may not be essential to making jewelry, but it is a must-have for designing custom pieces. Check out Chapter 4 to see what one looks like.

2. **Dig around in your bead stash to see what you have that may go with newfound beads.** Look for spacers to create space between the central beads. Look for coordinating beads that add the visual interest to your piece.

Look for both contrast and coordinating beads in terms of texture, shape, and color to vary the visual interest in your piece. A series of graduated round beads can work together, even if the colors are different. The shape pulls the design together. Maybe the colors of all your beads are in the same family, but the textures and shapes vary. Any combination can work. Let your imagination be your guide.

3. **Lay your possible selection on your bead board with the central beads and start to work on the design.** Play around with the arrangements of the beads. Look for patterns that work for you and those that don't.

Watch for and solve any physical problems with the central beads in this design phase. For example, the polymer clay beads in the patriotic necklace have huge (5mm+) stringing holes. When I started working with them, I realized that the holes would "swallow" the seed beads on the string, so I needed bead caps or another solution to keep the big beads in place and the small ones out in the open. I used giant spacer beads to both plug up the holes and add a cool feature to the necklace.

4. **Finalize your design.** After you've found patterns that you like, lay out the finished design on the bead board. Determine the length for the finished project and lay it out to match. Choose your findings to match the design.

5. **String it up.** Of course you may not be using string at all, but you get the picture. Move from the drawing board, or in this case the bead board, to an actual piece of finished jewelry. String, wrap, or thread the beads, depending on what your design calls for. Add the finishing touches and findings and enjoy your one-of-a-kind creation!

Designing for the Evening

I think jewelry designs for eveningwear should be glamorous, sparkling, and above all, fun. Occasionally, I make pieces for a particular outfit, picking up a color theme or pattern. But by nature, I'm a practical girl, so I like most of my jewelry to be independent from the outfit. (Interchangeability is a must!) All three projects in this section serve up glitz and glamour, but because they're classic, elegant styles, they go with just about anything. Feel free to alter lengths, color combinations, clasps, and anything else to make these designs your own.

Project 9-1: Crystal and Pearl Y-Necklace

This choker combines two trendy elements, a Y-necklace and a choker. I originally made this piece for a friend's wedding, but she likes it so much, she wears it often to formal events. Talk about versatility. It measures approximately 15 inches, but you can lengthen it or shorten it as you wish by removing equal numbers of beads from each side of the necklace. Check out Figure 9-3 for the finished necklace.

Tools and Materials

Round-nose pliers

Wire cutters

Crimp pliers (optional)

7 6mm faceted teardrop crystals, pendant drilled

31 4mm potato freshwater pearls, white, drilled side to side

47 5mm bicone crystals, clear AB finish

21 5mm 14kt gold daisy spacer beads

16 2mm smooth gold beads

2 2x2mm 14kt gold crimp beads

1 14kt gold toggle clasp

6 inches super fine 32-gauge beading wire, gold-colored

20 inches of nylon coated stainless steel beading wire, 0.10-inch diameter

1. **Thread 1 teardrop crystal onto the 32-gauge beading wire. Add a 2mm gold bead on each side of the teardrop. Fold the wire in half evenly. Then thread both ends through a single pearl.** Check out Figure 9-1a.

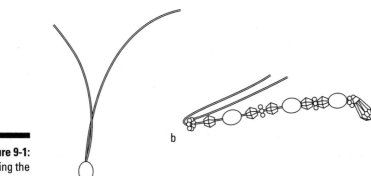

Figure 9-1:
Creating the "Y" dangle.

a

b

2. **Follow the pearl with the following pattern, threading both ends of the wire through each bead: bicone crystal, daisy spacer, bicone, pearl, bicone, daisy, bicone, pearl, bicone, daisy. Temporarily bend the wire to keep the bead from slipping off and set the component aside.** Check out Figure 9-1b.

3. **Slip 1 crimp bead onto the nylon coated beading wire. Follow it with one side of the toggle clasp. Reinsert the wire through the crimp bead to create a loop around the jump ring.** Take a look at Figure 9-2a. Using your crimp pliers, crimp the bead into place.

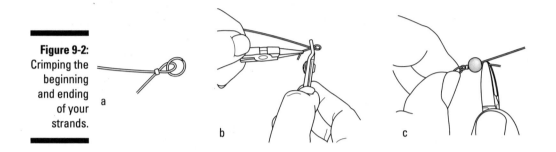

Figure 9-2:
Crimping the beginning and ending of your strands.

a

b

c

4. **Begin stringing your necklace following this pattern: gold bead, pearl, bicone, daisy, bicone, pearl, bicone, daisy, bicone, pearl, bicone, daisy, bicone, pearl, gold bead, teardrop crystal.**

5. **Repeat Step 4 five more times, but the third time, leave out the middle daisy spacer. Instead, you'll have 2 bicones right next to each other.** (This spot is the exact middle of your necklace. After you string the entire necklace, you'll go back and attach the component you created in Step 2 to this spot between these bicones to make the "Y.")

6. **Finish off your main strand of beads with the following pattern: gold bead, pearl, bicone, daisy, bicone, pearl, bicone, daisy, bicone, pearl, bicone, daisy, bicone, pearl, gold bead.**

7. **Slip 1 crimp bead onto the beading wire. Follow it with the remaining slide of the toggle clasp. Reinsert the wire through the crimp bead to create a loop around the clasp. With your crimp pliers, hold the crimp in place. Use your round-nose pliers to pull the wire tightly, taking up any slack in the necklace.** Take a look at Figure 9-2a and 9-2b. Using your crimp pliers, crimp the bead into place.

8. **Tuck the excess wire down into the first bead on the strand, and then trim the excess from the underside of the bead by using your wire cutters. Repeat this process with the other end of the necklace.** Check out Figure 9-2c.

9. **Find the middle point of your necklace (I identified it in Step 5). Take the component you created in Step 2 and create a wrapping loop (as shown in Chapter 7), but before you close the loop, attach it to your necklace between the two bicone beads that mark the middle point of your necklace.** See Figure 9-3 for a view of the finished project.

Figure 9-3:
Crystal and
Pearl Y-
Necklace.

Project 9-2: Alexandrite Surprise Necklace, Bracelet, and Earring Set

This choker, bracelet, and earring combination is sure to surprise and delight. The alexandrite appears light purple in normal light, but turns blue in fluorescent lights. Wear it dancing to amaze your friends under the different lighting conditions at the clubs. The bracelet measures approximately 7¼ inches, and the necklace is about 16 inches. See the completed project in Figure 9-4.

Tools and Materials

Round-nose pliers

Wire cutters

Crimp pliers (optional)

For the earrings:

2 leaverback earwires, sterling with a cut diamond shields design

6 6mm faceted round alexandrite Czech crystals

2 5mm round olive pearls

2 3-inch eye pins, sterling

2 1½-inch headpins, sterling

For the bracelet:

17 6mm faceted round alexandrite Czech crystals

15 5mm round olive pearls

1 1½-inch headpin, sterling

2 2x2mm crimp beads, sterling

1 jump ring, sterling

1 spring ring clasp, sterling

12 inches stainless steel coated nylon beading wire, 0.15-inch diameter

For the necklace:

35 6mm faceted round alexandrite Czech crystals

34 5mm round olive pearls

2 2x2mm crimp beads, sterling

2 jump ring, sterling

20 inches stainless steel coated nylon beading wire, 0.15-inch diameter

1 "S" clasp, sterling

1. **To make the earrings, string 3 beads in this order on an eyepin: 1 crystal, 1 pearl, 1 crystal. Using your round-nose pliers, begin to create a wrapping loop (see Chapter 7 for details), but connect it to one earwire before closing and wrapping the loop.**

2. **Thread one crystal onto an eye pin. Begin to create a wrapping loop, but connect it to the eyepin component before closing and wrapping the loop.**

3. **Repeat Steps 1 and 2 to create the second earring.**

4. **To make the bracelet, slip 1 crimp bead onto the beading wire. Follow it with a jump ring. Reinsert the wire through the crimp bead to create a loop around the jump ring.** Refer to Figure 9-2a. Use your round-nose pliers to hold the short end of the wire while you use your crimp pliers to crimp the bead into place. Refer to Figure 9-2b.

5. **Thread 1 crystal bead onto the wire. Tuck the excess wire down into this bead, and then trim the excess from the underside of the bead using your wire cutters.** Refer to Figure 9-2c.

6. **Thread the remaining beads onto the wire, alternating each crystal bead with a pearl. Continue stringing until you've used all your bracelet beads, except 1 crystal.** You should begin and end with a crystal.

7. **Slip one crimp bead onto the beading wire. Follow it with the spring ring clasp. Reinsert the wire through the crimp bead to create a loop around the clasp. With your crimp pliers, hold the crimp in place. Use**

your round-nose pliers to pull the wire tightly, taking up any slack in the bracelet. Using your crimp pliers, crimp the bead into place, as you did in Step 4.

8. **Tuck the excess wire down into the last bead on the strand, and then trim the excess from the underside of the bead, as you did in Step 5.**

    This step gives a clean finish to your strand and makes it look very professional.

9. **Slide the last crystal onto the headpin. Begin to create a wrapping loop, but connect it to the loop of the springring clasp before closing and wrapping the loop.** This step creates an elegant dangle at the clasp end of the bracelet.

10. **To make the necklace, repeat Steps 4 and 5 with the necklace beading wire.**

11. **Repeat Step 6, but use all the remaining beads.** You should begin and end your strand on a crystal.

12. **Repeat Step 7 with last jump ring and finish the end of the wire as in Step 8. Connect the two jump rings with the "S" clasp.**

Figure 9-4:
Alexandrite
Surprise
Necklace,
Bracelet,
and
Earring Set

Project 9-3: Uber-Long Crystal and Sterling Earrings

These earrings are quick to make, flashy, and unusual. If they feel a little long, feel free to shorten the chains. Also, feel free to vary the color to suit your taste. These are an excellent addition to any formal event. Check out the finished project in Figure 9-6.

Tools and Materials

Round-nose pliers	2 6mm bicone crystals, light amethyst
Wire cutters	2 6mm bicone crystals, ruby red
Jewelry file	2 6mm bicone crystals, zircon
2 earhooks, sterling	2 6mm bicone crystals, peridot
8 inches of medium weight link chain, sterling	8 1½-inch headpins, sterling

1. **Using your wire cutters, cut the chain into 2 pieces, each 4 inches long.**

2. **Gently open the loop of one earhook. Check out Figures 9-5a and 9-5b. Slip on one link of the chain. Check out Figure 9-5c. Gently re-close the loop. Repeat with the second earhook and piece of chain.**

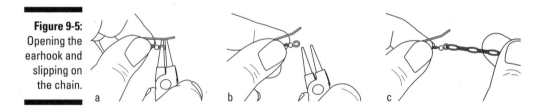

Figure 9-5: Opening the earhook and slipping on the chain.

a   b   c

3. **Slide 1 zircon crystal onto 1 headpin. Using your round-nose pliers, begin to create a wrapping loop (see Chapter 7 for details), but before closing the loop, insert the last link on the open end of one piece of chain.** Repeat this process with each color of crystal (light amethyst, ruby red, and peridot) on the same link of the same chain, as in Figure 9-6. File any sharp edges.

4. **Repeat Step 3 for the second earring.**

Figure 9-6:
Uber-Long
Crystal and
Sterling
Earrings.

Making the Bride Beautiful

Her wedding day is one of the most special days of a bride's life. Whether it's lacy and romantic, sleek and modern, or traditional, many times, a bride has some idea of what she wants to look like on her special day.

Here are a few specific questions to ask before designing a piece for a bride:

- **What does your dress look like?** You want information about the color, fabric, detailing, any beadwork, train, and so on. If you can actually see the dress, it's even better. You may notice design elements, like a beading pattern along a seam that the bride didn't mention.

- **What's kind of neckline does it show?** This question is important if you're designing a necklace. A straight across strapless gown is a great candidate for a shorter (16 inches or less) necklace or choker. A more plunging neckline may demand a longer piece, maybe with a pendant or lariat styling.

- **What color(s) do you want to emphasize?** If blush (light pink) and bashful (still light pink) are her signature colors, she may want you to design a piece around them.

✔ **If you're working with pearls, what shade and shape do you prefer?** Pearls come in just about every shade known to woman, but most of the time brides choose white or off-white. Don't take this for granted, though. Ask the question, don't assume. Check out Chapter 3 for information on the variety of shapes and colors of the world of pearls.

✔ **Do you prefer gold, silver, or some other metal?** Some brides want to match their accents to their wedding ring, screws in the church pews, or votive holders at the reception hall. Better safe than sorry, so just double check.

✔ **Are you wearing your hair up or down?** The answer can affect which clasp you choose and what kind of pattern to use near the clasp. If it's hidden by hair, you may be able to save a little money by repeating patterns of less expensive beads. But if she wears her hair up or has short hair, consider spending a bit more money on a beautiful clasp, like a toggle clasp with a heart-shaped lock and key.

✔ **What overall feel are you looking for?** If she's looking for lots of sparkle, think crystal. Or maybe she's looking for something more understated classic, consider pearls as your main design element. Or maybe she want to be somewhere in between? Let your imagination run wild.

✔ **How many pieces do you want?** Earrings only? A bracelet to match? The whole kit and caboodle?

✔ **What length should your pieces be?** This question is critical if you're working on a necklace. One bride may prefer opera length pearls, while another is expecting a choker. Make sure you determine the answer before you develop your design.

Project 9-4: Princess Pearls with Ribbon Necklace

Any bride will feel like a princess on her wedding day wearing this beautiful necklace. It's made from sterling silver chain, light and airy organza ribbon, and of course, crystals and pearls. Pair them with the earrings in Project 9-5 for a perfect wedding day look. Take a look at the finished project in Figure 9-8.

Tools and Materials

Round-nose pliers

Flat-nose pliers

Wire cutters

Scissors

2 pieces, 8 inches each, light pink ¼-inch-wide organza ribbon

2 pieces, 3 inches each, 22-gauge round wire, sterling, dead soft

2 1-inch cones, sterling

7¾ inch scallop chain, sterling

7 4mm white round pearls

7 4mm AB crystal cube beads

14 1½-inch headpins, sterling

2 8mm split jump rings, sterling

Hypo-cement

1 toggle clasp, sterling

1. **Fold 1 piece of ribbon and tie a knot in the end as close to the end of the ribbon as possible.** Trim away any excess ribbon.

2. **Use the round-nose pliers to make a small curl on the end of 1 wire.** This step helps you start wrapping around the knot on the ribbon.

3. **Put the wire curl around the end of the knot and use your flat-nose pliers to "smash" the wire around the ribbon. Continue to hold the wire with the pliers and use your fingers to wrap the wire around the rest of the knot, leaving about 1 inch of wire straight.** Check out Figure 9-7a.

4. **Place a dab of glue on the knot and insert the wire-wrapped knot through the wide end of the cone. The straight wire should be sticking out of the top of the cone.** See Figure 9-7b. Let the glue dry at least 10 minutes before proceeding.

5. **Begin making a wrapping loop (check out Chapter 7 for help) with the straight wire at the top of the cone, but before completing the loop, attach it to one side of the clasp.** Use wire cutters to trim excess wire, as necessary.

6. **Repeat Steps 1–5 with the second ribbon, the second piece of wire, the second cone, and the other side of the clasp.** Set the ribbon portion aside.

7. **Create a dangle using a headpin and crystal. Thread a crystal onto a headpin. Using your flat-nose and round-nose pliers, create an eye loop on the straight end of the headpin.** (See Chapter 7 for more on eye loops.) Before closing the eye loop, attach the dangle to the leftmost link of your scallop chain.

8. **Repeat Step 7 to complete the dangles, alternating between pearls and crystals, until you've completed Step 14.**

9. **Attach a jump ring to the last link of the scallop chain. Slide 1 ribbon component onto the jump ring, and then close it.** See Figure 9-7c.

10. **Repeat with the other end, attaching a jump ring and ribbon component.** See Figure 9-8 for a view of the finished project.

Figure 9-7:
Attaching the cones to the ribbon and the ribbon to the chain.

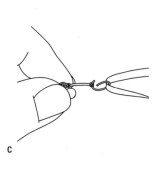

a

b

c

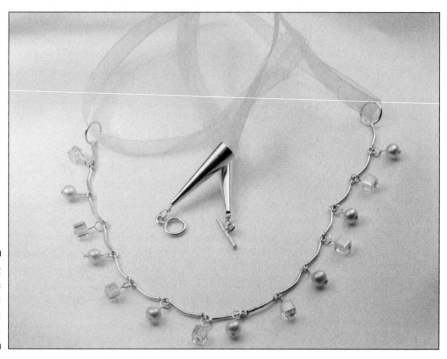

Figure 9-8:
Princess
Pearls with
Ribbon
Necklace.

Project 9-5: Bridal Earrings

These stunning earrings start with beautiful leaf-shaped leaverback earring findings. The leaf shape adds a dramatic touch to these delicate earrings. See the finished project in Figure 9-9.

Tools and Materials

Round-nose pliers

Wire cutters

Jewelry file

2 2-inch headpins, sterling silver

2 6mm AB clear cube crystals

2 10mm concentric circle charms with loop on each side, sterling silver

2 3-inch pieces of 24-gauge wire, sterling silver, half-hard

2 4mm round white pearls

2 leaf leaverback earring findings, sterling silver

1. Thread 1 crystal cube on a headpin. Use round-nose pliers to begin creating a wrapping loop (check out Chapter 7 for the steps to create a wrapping loop), but before completing the loop, attach it to one loop of one of the concentric circle charms. Complete and wrap the loop. Trim any excess wire from the loop. File down any sharp edges.

2. Thread 1 pearl on 1 piece of wire. Begin to create a wrapping loop, but before completing the loop, attach it to the other loop of the concentric circle charm from step one. Complete and wrap the loop.

3. Begin to create a wrapping loop on the straight end of the wire, but before completing the loop, attach it to the loop on the leaverback earring finding. Complete and wrap the loop. Trim any excess wire from the loop using your wire cutters. File down any sharp edges.

4. Complete Steps 1 through 3 to create the other earring.

Figure 9-9:
Bridal
Earrings
make a
great match
to the
Princess
Pearls with
Ribbon
Necklace.

Celebrating Holidays with Custom Jewelry and Beading projects

Holidays are a great opportunity to create customized jewelry. For adults and kids alike, make jewelry with any color combination or theme that works for your celebration. Check out Table 9-1 for ideas on customizing the projects in this section to meet your needs.

Table 9-1	Holiday Color Ideas	
Holiday	*Color Ideas*	*Design Thoughts*
Chanukah	Blue, silver	Stars, dreidel, menorah,
Chinese New Year	Red, orange, gold	Chinese symbols, lanterns, fish, flowers
Christmas	Red, green, silver, gold	Snowflakes, stars, crosses, Santa, stockings, reindeer
Day of the Dead	Purple, pink, white	Skeletons, flowers, prayer charms
Easter	Pastels	Eggs, bunnies, crosses
Halloween	Black, orange	Pumpkins, witches, monsters, gross
Kwanzaa	Red, green, black	Baskets, harvest symbols, African motifs
Valentine's Day	Red, pink, white	Hearts, flowers, candy

Project 9-6: Pumpkin Anklet

Celebrate a spooky holiday with a not-so-scary anklet. I used three pumpkin beads, but you could use any combination of Halloween themed beads that you like. Maybe candy corn, scarecrows, or ghosts are more your style. Customize away! Take a look at the way I finished the project in Figure 9-10.

Tools and Materials

Flat-nose pliers

Wire cutters

3 pumpkin lampwork beads

16 4mm orange bone beads

10 4mm black glass druk beads

48 size 11 green seed beads

14 inches green beading wire, 0.12-inch diameter

2 gold tone clamshell bead tips

1 gold tone jump ring

1 gold tone spring ring clasp

1. **Slip 1 clamshell onto your beading wire. Tie a knot on the wire, in the open clamshell. Close the clamshell around the knot.**

   I often double knot my wire, just to add a little security to the finished product. The clamshell covers it up, so why not?

2. **Begin string the beads onto the open end of your wire (the strung beads will rest on the clam shell) in the following order:**

   > 3 green seed beads
   >
   > 1 orange bone bead
   >
   > 3 green seed beads
   >
   > 1 orange bone bead
   >
   > 1 black druk bead
   >
   > 1 orange bone bead
   >
   > 3 green seed beads
   >
   > 1 orange bone bead
   >
   > 3 green seed beads
   >
   > 1 black druk bead
   >
   > 1 pumpkin lampwork bead
   >
   > 1 black druk bead

3. **Repeat Step 2 two more times. Then, complete the beading with the following beads:**

   > 3 green seed beads
   >
   > 1 orange bone bead
   >
   > 3 green seed beads
   >
   > 1 orange bone bead
   >
   > 1 black druk bead
   >
   > 1 orange bone bead
   >
   > 3 green seed beads
   >
   > 1 orange bone bead
   >
   > 3 green seed beads

4. **Slip a clamshell onto your wire. Tie a knot or two to secure the wire, use your wire cutters to trim any excess, and then clamp your clamshell over the knot.**

5. **Using your pliers, attach 1 clamshell to the jump ring and the other to the springring. Connect the springring and the jump ring together to complete the anklet.**

Figure 9-10:
Pumpkin
Anklet.

Project 9-7: Holiday Decoration

You can hang this from a tree or wrap around a candle or neck of a wine bottle and give as a gift. Vary the color scheme to use the design any time of the year. Check out Figure 9-12 for the finished decoration.

Tools and Materials

Round-nose pliers

1 surgical steel headpin

1 surgical steel eye pin

2 10mm red, green, and white lampwork beads

4 inches of ¼-inch wide sparkly white ribbon

Approximately 100 4mm red glass beads

Approximately 100 size 11 green seed beads

3 loops bracelet size memory wire

1. **Thread a 4mm red glass bead on the head pin. Follow with one lamp-work bead and another 4mm bead. Using your round-nose pliers, make a wrapping loop at the top of the headpin.** Set aside.

2. **Repeat Step 1 with the eye pin. Thread the white ribbon through the eye and tie a knot.** Set aside.

3. **Use round-nose pliers to form a loop at one end of the memory wire coil. Thread a 4mm red bead onto the coil. Follow it with a green seed bead. Repeat until you reach the end of the coil, finishing on a red bead.**

4. **Form a loop at the open end of the memory wire. Slip on the head pin component from Step1 before closing the loop. Bend the closed loop (with the component attached) at a 90-degree angle from the coils.** Check out Figure 9-11a and 9-11b for before and after illustrations.

Figure 9-11:
Bending a
90-degree
angle.

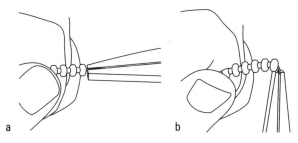

a   b

This step keeps all your beads right where you want them, on the coil, rather than all over the floor.

5. **Gently open the loop from the other end of the memory wire and slip on the eye pin and ribbon component from Step 2. Gently close the loop again. Bend the closed loop with the component on it at a 90-degree angle from the coils.** See Figure 9-12 for a view of the finished project.

If you prefer, you can also skip the ribbon and use another eyepin, instead. This variation gives you a more symmetrical look and saves you from working with ribbon.

Figure 9-12:
Holiday
Decoration.

Project 9-8: Holiday Chandelier Earrings

These earrings provide lots of glitz for very little effort. Spend money on the best crystals for optimal shine. Check out Figure 9-13 for the finished project.

Tools and Materials

Round-nose pliers

Flat-nose pliers

Wire cutters

2 5-loop chandelier earring compo-nents, sterling

2 ear hooks, sterling

10 1-inch headpins, sterling

6 6mm bicone ruby red crystals, AB finish

4 6mm bicone emerald green crystals, AB finish

1. **Thread 1 red crystal on a head pin. Connect it to the leftmost loop of one chandelier component by making an eye loop with your flat- and round-nose pliers (see Chapter 7), trimming any excess with wire cut-ters, as necessary.**

2. **Repeat Step 1 with green crystal, connecting the dangle to the next leftmost chandelier component. Continue alternating crystal colors until you reach the end of the component, finishing on a red dangle.** Set the chandelier component aside.

Figure 9-13:
Holiday
Chandelier
Earrings.

3. **With your round-nose pliers, gently open the loop on one earhook. Attach the chandelier component to the earhook. Gently close the loop again.**

4. **Repeat Steps 1 through 3 to create the second earring.**

Project 9-9: Freshwater Pearl and Rose Quartz Sweetheart Bracelet

This is the perfect item to wear or give to your sweetheart on Valentine's Day. Buy a few extra heart-shaped rose quartz beads to make a matching set of earrings. Figure 9-14 shows you the completed piece.

Tools and Materials

Scissors

Flat-nose pliers

#2 nylon thread- pink with needle attached

2 clamshell bead tips, sterling

2 rose quartz heart beads

42 4–5mm horizontally drilled, pear-shaped pearls

2 jump rings, sterling

1 lobster clasp, sterling

1. Thread 1 bead tip onto the thread. Next, string one rose quartz heart bead.

2. String all the pearls onto the thread. Follow with the last rose quartz heart bead.

3. Follow with a bead tip. Tie a knot inside the clamshell bead tip. Using your scissors, cut the thread close to the knot.

4. Close the bead tip around the knot, using your flat-nose pliers.

5. Repeat Steps 1 through 5 with the other end of the thread, making sure that the beads and bead tips are snug against each other as the knot is formed in the clamshell bead tip.

6. Attach a jump ring to the loop of 1 bead tip. Loop the other jump ring through the lobster clasp, and then attach this jump ring to the loop of the other bead tip.

Figure 9-14:
Freshwater
Pearl and
Rose Quartz
Sweetheart
Bracelet.

Project 9-10: Springtime Egg Stretch Bracelet

Stretchy bracelets are great because they're easy to wear for any age group, especially the oldest and youngest among us, who may have trouble working clasps with one hand. Create this super-springtime version in just a few minutes. It measures a little less than 8 inches in circumference. See Figure 9-15 for a look at the completed project.

Tools and Materials

Binder clip (from office supply store)

Scissors

12 inches 0.5 diameter clear elastic beading cord

6 15–16mm flat oval or egg shaped beads, drilled top to bottom, in spring-time colors (in my bracelet, 3 beads are pink, purple, and red, and the other 3 are yellow, green, and blue)

18 3mm round smooth gold beads

12 5mm round glass beads in coordi-nating springtime colors (I used 4 dif-ferent colors of swirly beads with pinks, purples, blues, greens, and yel-lows.)

Glue

1. **Clamp one end of the elastic cord with a binder clip.**

2. **String beads in the following pattern: oval bead, gold, round, gold, round, gold. Repeat this pattern five more times (six times total) to complete the stringing.**

3. **Carefully remove the binder clip from the elastic cord. Don't drop the end, or you'll lose all your hard work! Tie both ends of the cord together in a single knot. And because I'm probably overly cautious, I tie a second knot. Trim away the excess cord, but leave an ⅛ inch or so to help keep the knot in place.**

4. **Apply a dab of glue to the knot. Slide the knot inside the oval bead for a seamless look.** See Figure 9-15 for the finished product.

Figure 9-15:
Springtime
Egg Stretch
Bracelet.

Project 9-11: Patriotic Polymer Clay Necklace

This is a fun necklace to wear for all the patriotic holidays and observation days, including Independence Day, Veterans' Day, Memorial Day, Election Day(s), Arbor Day, President's Day, Flag Day, and so on. It measures approximately 18 inches and can also be worn on the wrist wrapped twice around as a loose, double strand bracelet. See the completed project in Figure 9-16.

Tools and Materials

Round-nose pliers

Wire cutters

Crimp pliers (optional)

5 18mm red, white, and blue polymer clay beads

14 5mm red glass druk beads48 clear seed beads, size 11

30 3mm blue glass druk beads

2 2x2mm sterling crimp beads

10 8mm daisy spacer beads, Bali style

1 large silver toggle clasp, Bali style

24 inches nylon wrapped stainless steel beading wire, 0.12-inch diamete

1. **Slip 1 crimp bead onto the beading wire. Follow it with one piece of the toggle clasp. Reinsert the wire through the crimp bead to create a loop around the clasp. With your crimp pliers, hold the crimp in place.**

Use your round-nose pliers to pull the wire tightly, making a small loop around the toggle clasp's connector loop. Refer to Figure 9-2b. Using your crimp pliers, crimp the bead into place.

2. **Begin stringing beads in the following order: blue, clear, blue, clear, blue, clear, red, clear.**

3. **Continue stringing beads in the following pattern: spacer, polymer bead, spacer, clear, red, clear, blue, clear, blue, clear, blue, clear, red, clear, blue, clear, blue, clear, blue, clear, red, clear. Repeat the pattern three more times.**

4. **Finish stringing the remaining beads in this order: spacer, polymer bead, spacer, clear, red, clear, blue, clear, blue, clear, blue.**

5. **Slip 1 crimp bead onto the beading wire. Follow it with the remaining piece of the toggle clasp. Reinsert the wire through the crimp bead to create a loop around the clasp. With your crimp pliers, hold the crimp in place. Use your round-nose pliers to pull the wire tightly, taking up any slack in the necklace.** Refer to Figure 9-2b. Using your crimp pliers, crimp the bead into place.

6. **Tuck the excess wire down into the first bead on the strand, and then use your wire cutters to trim the excess from the underside of the bead.** Refer to Figure 9-2c. Connect the end of your clasp together and bring on the fireworks!

Figure 9-16:
Patriotic
Polymer
Clay
Necklace.

Chapter 10

Making Jewelry with an Ethnic Feel

In This Chapter

▶ Getting to know African design trends

▶ Experimenting with Asian themes

▶ Knowing Native American jewelry elements

America is truly a melting pot. Most of us are transplants (somewhere along the line) from somewhere else. It's fun to show to celebrate cultural heritage, whether it's yours or someone else's.

In this chapter, I give you design ideas for celebrating the cultural heritage of two other continents, Africa and Asia. Then I show you how to have fun working with Native American designs. Read on for detailed projects and design ideas.

For even more cultural influences, check out Chapter 11. The last section in that chapter highlights design trends from Ancient Rome, Greece, and Egypt. And if you have any Irish ancestry (or even if you're Irish one day a year), also consider making the Celtic Wrapped Earrings (Project 7-4 in Chapter 7).

Identifying African Design Trends

Many people are familiar with the image of the African bead trader, trading strands of beads for everything from food to slaves. Africans were among first beaders in history using them to adorn cloaks and other clothing. Many African cultures today wear beautifully woven necklaces, headdresses, and arm and leg bands.

Make sure you check out Chapter 6 for information and projects covering bead weaving and beads.

Many African societies take jewelry as an adornment to an all-new level. People can wear only certain patterns or styles of jewelry at a certain stage of life, like during courtship, to celebrate an engagement, to signify the day of a marriage, or announce the birth of a child. Multiple strands of beads are worn at all different lengths by both men and women.

Africa is an incredibly diverse continent, so no generalization about what jewelry means in any society will be universal.

Common jewelry materials for African jewelry include clay, bone, horn, tusk, shell, stone, silver gold, coconut shell, seeds, and wood. Though many precious stones are mined in Africa, few are actually worn by the native population. More common though, are semi-precious stones like malachite, amazonite, amber, quartz, turquoise, and dolomite.

African designs influence everything from fashion to fine art, home décor, and jewelry. Many motifs and design elements make their way into jewelry and bead design including repetitive geometric patterns, animals, fish, crocodiles, turtles, moons, and carved masks.

To create an easy African-inspired necklace, get a selection of African trade beads, plus a carved mask pendant and string them up.

Project 10-1: African-Inspired Bracelet

This bracelet may not have a carved mask made from an elephant tusk, but it has African influences with the abundance of leopard-skin jasper. It measures approximately 7¼ inches long. See the finished project in Figure 10-1.

Tools and Materials

Wire cutters

Round-nose pliers

Flat-nose pliers

Bead board (optional)

Corsage pin

Approximately 7 inches of leopard-skin jasper chip beads

7 6mm amethyst round beads

10 inches of nylon coated stainless steel beading wire

Hypo-cement or glue of your choice

2 silvertone bead tips

1 silver tone spring ring clasp

1 silver tone jump ring

1¾-inch headpin, silvertone

1. **Arrange your beads on a bead board, if you're using one. Line up approximately ¾ inch of leopard skin beads on the board. Next, add an amethyst bead. Repeat this pattern, beginning and ending with the jasper beads. Set aside.** *Note:* You'll have one amethyst bead left over to make a pretty dangle in Step 9.

2. **Tie a knot close to the end of your beading wire. Tie a second knot right on top of it. Apply a dab of glue to the knots. Using your wire cutters, trim any remaining tail on the wire, so the knots are at the very end of your wire.**

3. **From the other end of the wire, string on your clamshell bead tip. Make sure you string it so that you can close the clamshell over the knots. Use your flat-nose pliers to close the clamshell.** The knots should be inside the clamshell.

4. **String the beads on in the order established in Step 1.**

5. **Slide on the remaining clamshell, with the opening of the shell facing away from the beads. Tie a loose knot in the remaining beading wire. Insert the corsage pin into the knot. Holding the thread in one hand and the pin in the other, tighten the knot by using the corsage pin to push the knot towards the inside of the clamshell.** Take a look at Chapter 5 if you need help with knotting.

6. **Repeat Step 5 to make a second knot. Place a dab of glue onto both knots. Trim away the excess wire using your wire cutters. Using your flat-nose pliers, close the clamshell around the knot.**

7. **Connect the loop of the clamshell to the jump ring. Using your flat-nose pliers, close the loop around the jump ring.**

8. **Repeat the process with the loop of the remaining clamshell and the springring clasp.**

9. **Slide the last amethyst bead onto the headpin. Using your round-nose pliers, begin to create a wrapping loop, but before closing the loop, slip the jump ring into the loop.** Check out Chapter 7 for help with wrapping loops.

Figure 10-1:
African-
Inspired
Bracelet.

Understanding Asian Influences

Many Asian cultures attach meaning to each stone and each carving of the stone. They choose to focus on protection, prosperity, wellness, good fortune, and happiness. Japanese and Chinese motifs include fish, dragons, symbols, written letters, and horoscope symbols, and each motif is tied to the hope of prosperity in one way or another.

Typical Asian material choices include jade, carved bone, cinnabar, jasper, carnelian, black onyx, quartz, cloisonné, red coral, and silver. Some regions are known for a particular material. For example, carnelian is closely tied with India. In fact, errant stones from lost ships, laden with carnelian and on their way from India to Africa; still show up on African shores.

Jewelry designers today use ancient pottery shards in modern-day settings to make pendants and dangles.

Project 10-2: Japanese-Inspired Jade Pendant Necklace

This necklace is made from jade and cloisonné, two very typical components in Asian jewelry. It measures approximately 22 inches long — see the finished necklace in Figure 10-3. Wear it for long life and fertility!

Tools and Materials

Wire cutters

Round-nose pliers

Flat-nose pliers

Jewelry files

Crimp pliers (optional)

Bead board (optional)

1 50mm Jade doughnut

12 inches 20-gauge gold-filled round wire, half-hard

26 inches nylon coated stainless steel beading wire, 0.12-inch diameter

1 14kt gold-filled toggle clasp

2 2x2mm crimp beads, gold

66 5mm round jade beads

16 5mm daisy spacer beads 18kt gold

20 2mm 18kt gold round beads

4 10mm round cloisonné beads, red, gold, and green

6 5mm round cloisonné beads, red, gold, and green

1. **Thread the gold-filled wire through the center of the doughnut. Fold the wire in half around the doughnut, as shown in Figure 10-2a.**

2. **Using the first wrap as a center point, continue wrapping the wire around the doughnut several times, moving out from the center. Leave approximately 1½ inches of wire on one side and 2½ inches on the other.** Take a look at Figure 10-2b.

3. **Use the longer side of the gold-filled wire to create a large wrapping loop. This loop will serve as the bail for your pendant. Wrap the wire**

around both end wires. Continue wrapping the shorter end to line up with the wrap you already started. Trim away any excess and file the ends smooth. Set aside. Take a look at Figure 10-2c to see the finished pendant component.

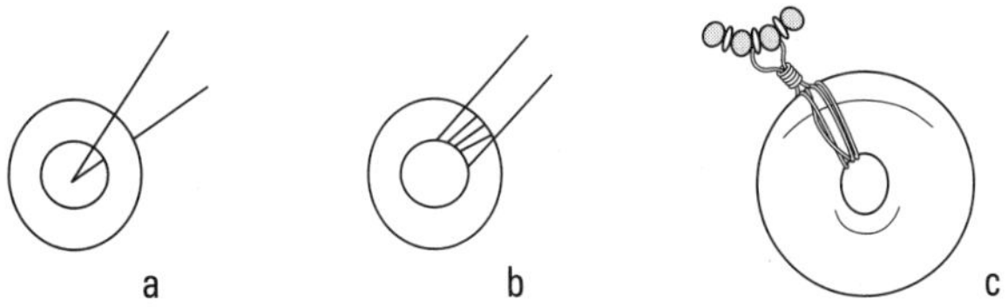

Figure 10-2:
Wrapping
wire around
a doughnut
to create
a bail.

a   b   c

4. **Thread a crimp bead onto your beading wire. Follow it with one side of your toggle clasp. Rethread the beading wire though the crimp bead. Using your crimp pliers, crimp the bead in place.** Take a look at Chapter 2 if you need help with this step.

5. **Begin stringing beads in the following order:** 3 jade, 1 daisy, 2 jade, 1 daisy, 2 jade, 1 gold ball, 1 small cloisonné, 1 gold ball, 2 jade, 1 daisy, 2 jade, 1 daisy, 2 jade, 1 gold ball, 1 large cloisonné, 1 gold ball, 2 jade, 1 daisy, 2 jade, 1 gold, 1 small cloisonné, 1 gold ball, 2 jade, 1 daisy, 4 jade, 1 daisy, 2 jade, 1 gold ball, 1 small cloisonné, 1 gold ball, 2 jade, 1 gold ball, 1 large cloisonné, 1 gold ball, 5 jade, 1 daisy, 1 jade. This is the center point of your necklace.

I recommend that you lay out this pattern along one side of your bead board, and then mirror it on the other side. Your pendant will lay directly at the center point. A bead board really helps you work on symmetrical designs even when you're not designing a piece, per se. It allows you to lay out your pattern, count your beads, and make sure you have what you need where you need it. Then you can string your piece up with few, if any, errors.

6. **Slip on the pendant. Then repeat the pattern from Step 5 backward, starting with a single jade bead and ending with three jade beads.** Again, this is much easier if you lay your design out on your bead board before you start stringing.

7. **Slide a crimp bead on the beading wire. Follow it with one side of your toggle clasp. Rethread the beading wire though the crimp bead. Hold the crimp bead gently with your crimp pliers. Using your other hand, pull the wire taught to take up any slack in your necklace. Then crimp your bead into place. Thread the end wire down through the first bead on your strand. Using your wire cutters, cut off any excess wire under your first bead.** This step gives your necklace a more finished and professional look. Take a look at Chapter 9 to see what this technique looks like.

Figure 10-3:
Japanese-
Inspired
Jade
Pendant
Necklace.

Project 10-3: Asian-Inspired Good-Luck Necklace and Earrings

Red is considered a lucky color in Asian cultures. It means prosperity and brings a re-energizing spirit. On the New Year, Chinese people give each other red envelopes with money, in the hope that they will have a prosperous year. I hope that spirit stays with you as you wear this necklace and earrings combo. See Figure 10-5.

Tools and Materials

Wire cutters

Round-nose pliers

Flat-nose pliers

Scissors

Jewelry files

For the necklace:

36 inches, red suede cord, 3mm wide

1 round replica Chinese coin with center hole, 25mm diameter

1 18mm x 60mm rectangular replica Chinese coin with top hole

For the earrings:

10 inches 21-gauge gold-filled round wire, half-hard

2 round replica Chinese coins with center holes, 25mm diameter

2 6mm bicone ruby red AB crystals

2 gold-filled ear hooks

1. **Fold the suede in half. Insert the folded end through the hole in the round coin, as shown in Figure 10-4a.**

2. **Slip the rectangular coin onto one strand of the suede.** Check out Figure 10-4b to see how this looks.

3. **Push the rectangular coin down toward the round coin. Then insert both ends of sued through the loop of suede created in Step 1.** Figure 10-4c shows you how.

Figure 10-4:
Tying the suede around the coins to create a pendant.

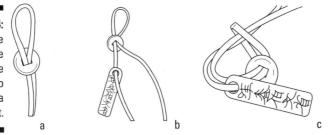

a   b   c

4. **Pull suede tight and coins together. Finish the end with an overhand knot and trim excess suede.** Figure 10-5 shows you the finished necklace and earrings.

Figure 10-5:
Asian-Inspired Good-Luck Necklace and Earrings.

5. To make the earrings, cut the gold-filled wire into two equal pieces, each approximately 5 inches in length.

6. Thread 1 piece of wire through the center of one coin. Bend it so that about 1½ inches are on one side of the coin and 3½ inches are on the other side, as shown in Figure 10-6a.

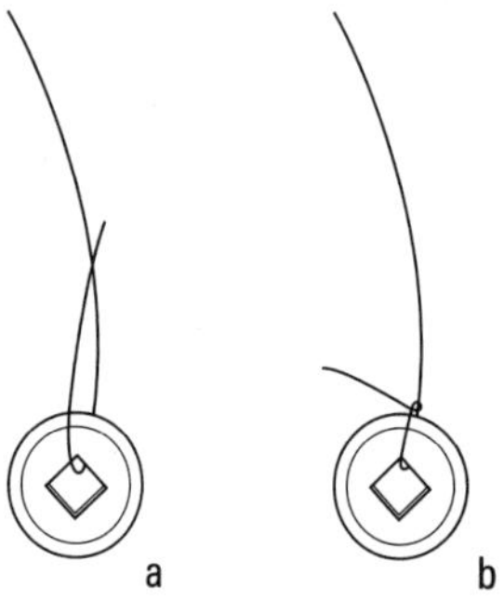

Figure 10-6:
Wrapping
wire around
the replica
Chinese
coin.

a   b

7. Using your round- and flat-nose pliers, make a wrapping loop, with the loop going through the center of the coin. Take a look at Figure 10-6b. (Check out Chapter 7 if you need help with wrapping loops.) Make 3 or so even, tight wraps with the shorter end of the wire, and then trim the excess with your wire cutters, leaving the long end intact. File the end of the cut wire smooth.

8. Slide 1 crystal down the straight end of the wire. Begin to make a wrapping loop on this end of the wire, but before you close the loop, slide the ear hook onto the wire. Make 3 or so even, tight wraps, and then trim the excess. File the end smooth.

9. Repeat Steps 6 through 8 for the second earring. Refer to Figure 11-5 to see the final pieces, paired with a matching necklace.

Project 10-4: Indian-Inspired Chandelier Earrings

I love these Indian-inspired earrings, shown completed in Figure 10-8. I ran into some trouble with a strand of glass beads that I bought and loved. The beading holes are extremely small, making it tough (actually, impossible) to string on headpins or eyepins, even with the help of a bead reamer. So instead of head-pins, I made strands of beads on super-fine beading wire, ran it through a clamshell finding, and — voila! — custom-made headpins.

TIP

If you're using beads with larger bead holes, feel free to use headpins. You'll need 2-inch headpins (instead of the super-fine beading wire), and you can leave the clamshells off your supply list. Add round-nose pliers to your tools list so you can make loops in your headpins.

Tools and Materials

Wire cutters

Flat-nose pliers

2 leaverback earring findings, sterling

2 3-hoop chandelier findings, sterling

2 split jump rings, sterling

6 pieces 6 inches each 32-gauge super-fine beading wire

6 3mm antiqued metal beads

12 8mm Bali-style tube beads, sterling

18 5mm rectangle glass beads, (6 each purple, yellow, and green)

6 8mm Bali-style flower spacer beads

6 clamshell bead tips, sterling

1. **Create the bead dangles first. String 1 antiqued metal bead on 1 piece of super fine beading wire. Fold the wire in half, with the bead resting in the loop, as shown in Figure 10-7a.** This bead acts as the head of a headpin to hold the beads on the dangle.

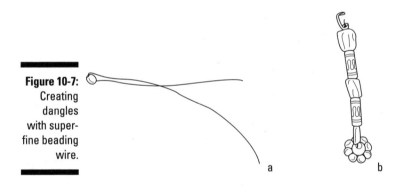

Figure 10-7:
Creating dangles with super-fine beading wire.

a   b

2. **Thread both strands of the beading wire up through a flower spacer bead. Slide the spacer as close to the antiqued metal bead as possible. Follow the spacer with beads in the following order: green, tube, yellow, tube, purple.** Each time you string a bead, slide it down next to the previous bead for a tight fit.

3. **Slide both ends of the wire up through the whole in the clamshell. Tie an overhand knot in the beading wire. Follow it with a second knot. With your wire cutters, trim off excess beading wire. Using your flat-nose pliers, close the clamshell around the knot. (The knot will be inside the clamshell.)** Your dangle should look like Figure 10-7b. Set aside.

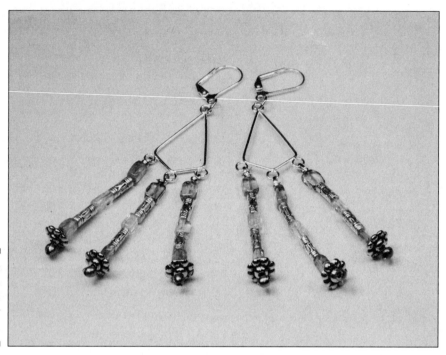

Figure 10-8:
Indian-
Inspired
Chandelier
Earrings.

4. **Repeat Steps 1 through 3 five more times to create a total of six dangles.**

5. **Connect the dangle to one hoop of one chandelier finding. Close the loop around the hoop with your flat-nose pliers.** Repeat with the remaining dangles and hoops.

6. **Use a jump ring to connect the chandelier finding to the leverback earring finding. Use your flat-nose pliers to open the jump ring. Slide the loop on the leverback onto the jump ring. Slide the top loop of the chandelier finding onto the jump ring. Gently close the jump ring with your flat-nose pliers.** Check out Chapter 7 if you need help opening and closing jump rings.

Creating Native American–Inspired Jewelry

The Native American tribes of the American Southwest spawned a design trend in this country, often called Southwestern jewelry. It's typified by the kind of stones used in it, typically turquoise, malachite, lapis lazuli, and sugilite. More often than not, these stones are paired with sterling silver.

Southwestern designs tend to incorporate natural looking stones. Stone shapes are usually nuggets and chips, rather than faceted and highly polished pieces. Typical motifs include animal-inspired elements (like feathers, bears, bear claws, buffalos, eagles, and roadrunners), natural elements (like the moon, sun, water, and earth), everyday life items (like arrowheads, hunting, or cooking), and spiritual elements (usually symbols that show life's journey, the Great Spirit, and the like).

Project 10-5: Native American–Inspired Necklace

Turquoise is an important stone in many Native American jewelry styles. I've included this piece (shown completed in Figure 10-9) to give you an option that's not so Southwestern-feeling, but still uses Native American elements. It measures approximately 20 inches long.

Tools and Materials

Wire cutters

Flat-nose pliers

Crimp pliers

Bead board

7 inches of lapis lazuli chip beads

3 large (approximately 14–18mm) turquoise oval beads

10 8mm round tiger's eye beads

6 4mm round tiger's eye beads

36 4mm dark amethyst Czech crystals, AB finish

1 toggle clasp, sterling

2 2x2mm crimp beads, sterling

24 inches of nylon coated stainless steel beading wire, 0.12-inch diameter

REMEMBER

1. **Arrange your beading pattern on your bead board. Place 1 turquoise bead at the zero point (center) of your necklace tray on your bead board. Place an amethyst crystal on either side followed by a large tiger's eye bead and another amethyst crystal.**

   You're building your design from the center out, working both sides at the same time to create a symmetrical design.

2. **Add ½ inch of lapis chips (approximately 3 chips though size of chips will vary) next to the amethyst crystals. Follow them with another amethyst, small tiger's eye, and another amethyst. Next add another ½ inch of lapis chips, amethyst crystal, large tiger's eye, and an amethyst crystal.**

3. **Add 1 large turquoise bead to each side of your design. Follow each with an amethyst crystal.**

4. **Follow each amethyst crystal with a large tiger's eye, an amethyst crystal, and ⅓ inch of lapis chips. Add an amethyst crystal, small tiger's eye, an amethyst crystal, and ½ inch of lapis chips.**

5. **Repeat Step 4.**

6. **Add an amethyst crystal, small tiger's eye, and an amethyst crystal to complete the design.** Set your bead board aside.

7. **Slide a crimp bead onto your beading wire. Follow it with the loop from 1 piece of your toggle clasp. Rethread the wire through the crimp bead, making loop with the wire that holds the loop on your clasp. Using your crimp pliers, crimp the bead in place.** Check out Chapter 2 if you need help with this technique.

8. **Begin stringing your beads onto your wire. Start at one end (amethyst crystal) and work your way to the very last bead at the other end (amethyst crystal).**

When stringing your beads, work from end to end. When building your design on the bead board, work from the middle out.

Try to tuck the end of the beading wire into the first few beads. This step gives your strand a finished, professional look.

9. **After all of your beads have been strung, slide a crimp bead on the beading wire. Follow it with the other side of your toggle clasp. Rethread the beading wire though the crimp bead. Hold the crimp bead gently with your crimp pliers. Using your other hand and your flat-nose pliers, pull the wire taut to take up any slack in your necklace. Then crimp your bead into place. Thread the end wire down through the first bead on your strand. Using your wire cutters, cut off any excess wire under your first bead.** Take a look at Chapter 9 to see what this technique looks like.

Figure 10-9:
Native
American–
Inspired
Necklace.

Project 10-6: Native American Bear and Bone Necklace

My daughter Riley designed this necklace, shown completed in Figure 10-10. She designed it to give to a school friend for his birthday. Change the pendant to give the necklace a more or less masculine feel. The original necklace sported a very cool wolf pendant, in honor of the favorite animal of the birthday boy.

Because this was designed for a child, it's only about 14 inches long. Feel free to add additional repetitions of the primary pattern (1 bone tube, 3 heishe disks) to lengthen it. Each repetition is about 1¼ inches. If you want to lengthen it in smaller increments, add heishe disks between the bone beads or near the clasp. Just make sure to keep the design symmetrical. Use a bead board if you need to.

Tools and Materials

Wire cutters

Flat-nose pliers

Crimp pliers

18 inches of nylon coated stainless steel beading wire, 0.12 diameter

42 (roughly 3½ inches) 5mm heishe disk beads, shell

10 25mm carved tube beads, simulated bone, off-white

1 bear pendant

2 antiqued metal beads

2 2x2mm crimp beads

1 barrel clasp

1. **Slide a crimp bead onto your beading wire. Follow it with the loop from one piece of your barrel clasp. Rethread the wire through the crimp bead, making loop with the wire that holds the loop on your clasp. Using your crimp pliers, crimp the bead in place.** Check out Chapter 2 if you need help with this technique.

2. **Slide on one antiqued bead. Tuck the end of the beading wire (below the crimp) into the antiqued bead.**

3. **String 5 heishe disks onto your beading wire.**

4. **Follow it with a bone tube and 3 heishe disks.**

5. **Repeat Step 4 four more times for a total of five.** This brings you to the center point of your necklace.

6. **Slide on your bear pendant. Follow the pendant with 3 heishe disks.**

7. **Add 1 bone tube and 3 heishe disks. Repeat the 1 bone tube, 3 heishe disks pattern four times for a total of 5 times.**

8. **Add 2 more heishe disks and an antiqued bead to finish your stringing.**

9. **Slide a crimp bead on the beading wire. Follow it with the remaining side of your barrel clasp. Rethread the beading wire though the crimp bead. Hold the crimp bead gently with your crimp pliers. Using your other hand and your flat-nose pliers, pull the wire taut to take up any slack in your necklace. Then crimp your bead into place. Thread the end wire down through the first bead on your strand. Using your wire cutters, cut off any excess wire under your first bead.** Take a look at Chapter 9 to see what this technique looks like.

Figure 10-10:
Native
American
Bear and
Bone
Necklace.

Chapter 11

Getting that Retro Look: Inspirations for Making the New Look Old

In This Chapter

▶ Using retro styles in your jewelry today

▶ Borrowing design ideas from ancient history

*F*or at least 15,000 years, people have been wearing jewelry. (You can't get more retro than that!) In the earliest times, beads were used for adornment; later, they indicated the wearer's status within the community.

This chapter takes inspiration from more recent examples, like select decades from the last century. I select five separate decades and give you design hints and projects to match the then au courante fashions. Finally, I take you a bit further back in time, back to Ancient Greece, Rome, and Egypt, to get an overview of what how today's jewelry trends take their cues from pre-modern times.

Using Classic Design Principles to Create New Jewelry

As with textile fashion, jewelry from most time periods evokes a certain set of images. Often, those images are an exaggeration of a few elements that were popular at that time. For example, a few people in the 1950s actually wore poodle skirts and a few people have massive amounts of body piercings today. We remember the poodle skirts, and it will be hard to forget the belly button rings.

In fact, often when you create jewelry with the feel of a time period, it may seem to capture the essence of an era better than an authentic item from the time period. The human memory is sketchy at best. It remembers icons even if those icons are only a small part of the larger whole.

Here are my tips for making retro-inspired creations today:

- ✔ **Accentuate accessories.** Consider whether the time period was known for particular accessories that were bejeweled, bedazzled, or beaded. The 1890s sported some high collars, just ripe for the addition of cameos. The hats of the 1940s scream for hat pins. And the top-buttoned crisp collars of the 1980s need a pearl studded pin. (My motto is "What works for Molly Ringwald works for me.")

- ✔ **Consider color.** Many time periods are known for their use of particular colors (or combinations of color). The 1960s were known for solid, bright colors, like oranges, pinks, and greens. The 1940s saw muted colors like ambers, browns, burnt sienna, umber, grays, and black. Neon defined the 1980s. And what would the grunge-filled 1990s have been without plaid? (Okay, not exactly a color, but you get the picture.) If you're designing a piece from that time period, make sure your colors are in the palette of the time period.

- ✔ **Size-up shapes.** Many periods were known for particular kinds of shapes. Most cameos from the turn of the century were ovals, regardless of the size. The 1960s emphasized true geometric shapes like circles, squares, and triangles. And the 1970s took all those shapes and stretched and smashed them. Consider how the shape of an era should impact your design.

- ✔ **Mull over motifs.** Motifs are visual themes that show up in a certain style of jewelry making.

- ✔ **Set your sights on style.** Different styles of jewelry make appearances throughout history. The charm bracelet has been in and out of fashion for many years. The turn of the century pieces often were threaded on a simple ribbon. 1920s' styles became tasseled and dangly as dresses became more revealing. Look at old pictures, magazines, and movies to get an idea of what styles were popular during different eras.

- ✔ **Look at the length.** I've heard it said that necklaces get longer as hemlines get shorter; someday they'll meet around the belly button. Now, I don't have any data to back that up, but it's the kind of thing that I look at when designing retro jewelry. Consider what lengths were hip during the time period you're designing for.

Project 11-1: 1920s-Inspired Tassel Necklace

The tassel necklace is long, about 30 inches, and is the perfect accessory for your flapper. Because it's so long, you can easily slip it over your head, so no clasp is require. In this project, I give you general guidelines rather than hard fast directions, so enjoy making your personalized creation. I show you mine in Figure 11-3.

Tools and Materials

Scissors

Corsage pin

1 card size 2 nylon thread with attached needle

1 large bead (about 20mm)

2 medium beads (about 15mm), dark brown semi-transparent

1 small (6–8mm) transparent light brown round bead

Approximately 400 clear seed beads, size 8

Approximately 30 bugle beads, metallic brown

8 sets 2 each of 8mm glass and/or stone beads in coordinating colors

Approximately 15 3–4mm faceted Czech crystals in coordinating colors

Glue

1. **To make the fringe strand, thread on you choice of seed beads, bugles, and other beads (such as Czech crystals) onto the nylon thread. Make a strand approximately 3 inches long. Push the strand of beads all the way down so they're approximately 3 inches from the end of the card of thread.**

   Make sure the last bead you string on your strand of fringe is a seed bead. It serves to anchor the beads in the strand, like sort of the flat end of a head pin for the fringe.

2. **Slide the last bead up the thread slightly and thread the needle back through the other beads in the strand. You should finish with the string coming out the same bead you started stringing through. Pull the thread so that the strand has no gaps between the beads.** Take a look Figure 11-1a to see what your fringe should look like.

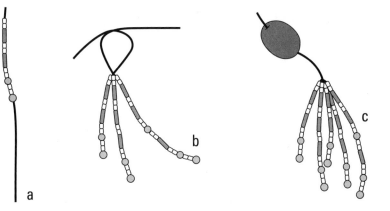

Figure 11-1:
Creating
the tassel.

a

b

c

3. **Tie an overhand knot close to the first bead on the strand and repeat to add as many fringes as you like. Tie a knot in between each piece you add. (I made five pieces.) Vary the length slightly to create additional**

visual interest in the piece. I recommend that you keep the length on the tassels between 3 and 4½ inches. See Figure 11-1b for help.

4. Gather your fringe together and tie a number of overhand knots in the collective threads. Dab a little glue on the knot.

5. Next, slip on your large bead and slide it down so it covers your knot at the top of your fringe. This is tassel of your necklace. Take a look at Figure 11-1c.

6. Slip the smaller bead onto the thread. Add a few inches of spacer beads (such as seed and bugle beads). I created a pattern of sorts by adding 10 seeds beads, a tube bead, and then 10 more seed beads.

7. Next add one medium bead and continue to add 24 inches of beads in your choice of designs. I recommend that you keep your design *symmetrical,* or the same on both sides of the necklace.

One way to balance the symmetry of the design with the ease of a bead board it to layout just your medium beads on the board. Choose a number of seed beads to string between the medium beads. Then start counting. String 10 seed beads, and then string the next medium bead on the board. Repeat. Remember that you are working from the tassel (in the bottom center of your necklace), going around the length of the necklace, and ending back at the tassel.

9. After you've created approximately 24 inches (not including the tassel) of strung beads, slip your needle down through the small bead resting on top of the tassel. Check out Figure 11-2.

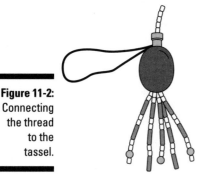

Figure 11-2:
Connecting
the thread
to the
tassel.

10. Make an overhand knot and use the corsage pin inserted through the knot to push the knot up close to the large bead. Make another knot and dab glue on the knot.

11. Slip the needle down through the large bead and trim off the excess nylon.

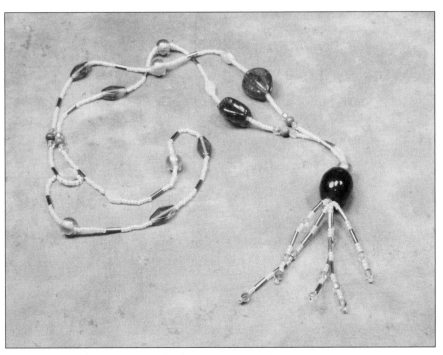

Figure 11-3:
1920s-
Inspired
Tassel
Necklace.

Project 11-2: 1940s-Inspired Garnet Hat Pin

In the 1940s, hats were all the rage. A lady wasn't properly dressed without one. So it's no surprise that people wanted to accessorize with this must-have accessory. Create a 1940s feel with this hat pin. If you don't have an occasion to wear a hat, it makes a beautiful lapel pin as well. Take a look at the finished piece in Figure 11-4.

Tools and Materials

Crimp pliers (you could use flat-nose pliers if you prefer)

1 gold-filled 3x2mm crimp bead

1 5-inch gold-colored stick pin

1 gold-colored clutch (special finding for the bottom of a stick pin)

2 12mm topaz-colored Czech Fire Polished Crystals

1 garnet vermeil bead

1. **Slide the beads on the stick pin in this order: 1 topaz crystal, the garnet vermeil bead, 1 topaz crystal.**

2. **Slide the crimp bead onto the stick pin. Add the clutch to keep from poking yourself. (Maybe it's just me, but I'm bound to draw blood without this step.) Turn the stickpin upside down so that all the beads are stacked tightly without any spaces between them.**

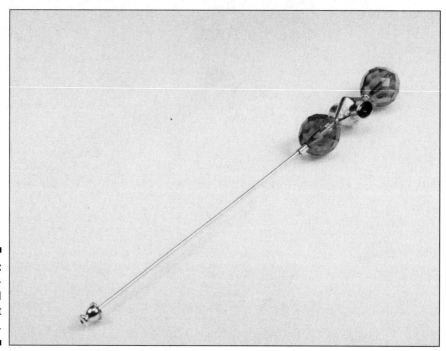

Figure 11-4:
1940s-
Inspired
Garnet
Hat Pin.

3. **Using your pliers, smash the crimp bead around the stick pin to hold the beads in place. Turn the pin right side up and enjoy your beautiful new heirloom.**

The beads can spin around on this pin. If you'd prefer them to stay in place, add a dab of Hypo-cement to each bead.

Project 11-3: 1950s-Inspired Rat Pack Charm Bracelet

Since the 1950s, the charm bracelet's made a lasting impact on the American scene. While this decade didn't see the first charm bracelets in history, it became the must-have item for many women, teenagers, and little girls. Pair that trend with the glamour of Hollywood and the celebrity of the Rat Pack, and you pay homage to an unforgettable decade with this charm bracelet. Take a look at the finished project in Figure 11-5.